T0164629

"Maggie Scarf brings laser-like powers of perception to bear in *The Remarriage Blueprint*, and the result is a compelling survey of how different couples handle the challenges—and opportunities—that come with second (or third) marriages. The combination of riveting personal stories and practical knowledge makes this book a must-read."

—Letty Cottin Pogrebin, founding editor of *Ms.* magazine
and author of *How To Be a Friend To a Friend Who's Sick*

"As a couple and family therapist, I've often wondered how the unresolved issues that couples bring to second marriages get played out. Through her thought-provoking interviews, Maggie Scarf sheds new light on these processes, as well as the ways in which second marriages create entirely new issues for such couples to tackle."

—Hannah Fox, director of the Met Center for
Object-Relations Theory and Practice and
professor at NYU Graduate School of Social Work

"Maggie Scarf tells the stories of seven very different remarried couples and masterfully captures the details of each family's triumphs and struggles. This is a rich, thoughtful book, written with clarity and compassion."

—Dr. Patricia L. Papernow, author of *Surviving and Thriving
in Stepfamily Relationships: What Works and What Doesn't*
and *Becoming a Stepfamily*

"The dilemmas of remarriage have received little attention compared with the abundance of literature on divorce and separation. This lucid, well-researched book will correct that deficiency. It should be required reading for those contemplating remarriage and for therapists, lawyers, judges, and extended families who are the advisers, supporters, and decision makers for these families."

—Carol C. Nadelson, MD, professor of psychiatry,
Harvard Medical School

"Invaluable insight for anyone contemplating or struggling with remarriage. Scarf helps readers face the illusions, secrets, conflicting cultures, money problems, and (especially) difficulties of stepparenting that can distort the structure of family life. An extremely helpful book on a topic that receives too little attention."

—Peter D. Kramer, clinical professor of psychiatry and human behavior at Brown University and author of *Listening to Prozac*

"For people ready to try it again, this time with their eyes open, Maggie Scarf's thoughtful book is a sober and sobering exploration of the pitfalls as well as the satisfactions of remarriage."

—Alix Kates Shulman, author of *A Marriage Agreement and Other Essays*

"Ever since its medieval debut in *The Book of Common Prayer*, the wedding vow has warned couples what marriage can bring—poverty, illness, and a bucket list of what turns out worse instead of better. Does hard-won experience make a second, or a third, attempt at wedlock more successful? Articulate, compassionate, and wise, Maggie Scarf has placed herself between fresh hopes and, sometimes, new disappointments to come back with a guide for the perplexed."

—Kathryn Harrison

THE
REMARRIAGE
BLUEPRINT

HOW REMARRIED COUPLES AND
THEIR FAMILIES SUCCEED OR FAIL

MAGGIE SCARF

SCRIBNER

New York   London   Toronto   Sydney   New Delhi

Scribner
A Division of Simon & Schuster, Inc.
1230 Avenue of the Americas
New York, NY 10020

First Scribner trade paperback edition August 2014

SCRIBNER and design are registered trademarks of The Gale Group, Inc.,
used under license by Simon & Schuster, Inc., the publisher of this work.

For information about special discounts for bulk purchases,
please contact Simon & Schuster Special Sales at 1-866-506-1949
or business@simonandschuster.com.

The Simon & Schuster Speakers Bureau can bring authors to your live event.
For more information or to book an event, contact the Simon & Schuster Speakers Bureau
at 1-866-248-3049 or visit our website at www.simonspeakers.com.

Manufactured in the United States of America

3   5   7   9   10   8   6   4   2

Library of Congress Control Number: 2012046790

ISBN 978-1-4391-6954-4
ISBN 978-1-4391-6955-1 (ebook)

Names and identifying details of some individuals in this book have been changed.

*This book is dedicated to
the many courageous and forthright couples
who volunteered to share their most intimate
life stories with me.*

Table of Contents

Prologue: In Unknown Territory   1

1. The Myth of Instant Love: Julie and Matthew Albright,
1997 and 2009   19

    The Albrights in 1997   19

    The Albrights in 2009   32

2. Constructing the Architectural Model   53

3. A New Life: Sara and Cliff Duvalier, 2009–2010   81

4. Soft Hard-Soft: Owen and Abbie Jamison, 2010   103

5. Patterns of the Past: Greg and Caroline Meyer, 2011   117

6. Boundless Trust: Carole and Ted Burke, 1997 and 2010   135

    The Burkes in 1997   135

    The Burkes in 2010   151

7. Wedding Bells and Dollar Bills   169

8. Across Cultures: Miguel Perez and Vicki de Matteo,
2010   183

9. A Charmed Life: Margaret and Bruce Gray, 2011   201

    Epilogue   219

    Acknowledgments   225

    Suggested Further Reading and Resources   227

    Q&A with Maggie Scarf   229

THE
REMARRIAGE
BLUEPRINT

In Unknown Territory

A common way of picturing remarriage is as a freshly cleaned slate, a new chance at happiness in a completely different relationship. The remarrying pair typically set out with a sense of optimism, a belief that *this* marriage will improve the quality not only of their own lives but the lives of the children involved. It just seems obvious, from the point of view of both emotional and economic resources, that having two concerned adults on the scene will double the family's store of available supplies.

The remarrying partners are also hoping to give their children the opportunity to grow up in the kind of happy, harmonious family environment that can be created only by relatively contented, mutually loving mates. *This* time around, the members of the pair believe, they can circumvent or completely avoid the blunders and disasters they encountered earlier. After all, both are now somewhat older and more self-knowledgeable. They feel far more competent when it comes to choosing the "right" kind of partner and a much greater readiness to make the necessary compromises that being in a close attachment requires.

Still, despite all their accrued wisdom and life experience, the new mates will not be fully aware of the complex challenges involved in putting the parts of their two former families together. Although they themselves may be embarking upon the marriage with the delicious feelings of increased energy and self-worth that being in a loving, intimate relationship can bring, they will rarely progress very far before finding themselves faced with dilemmas that are so dissimilar from anything that either faced in his or her first marriage that they may soon be feeling that they are traveling in an uncharted region without a clue about where they are and where they may be heading. What they need most is to be forewarned and educated about the typical kinds of surprises and challenges they will confront in the course of journeying toward their ultimate destination: that of becoming a unified "we," an emotionally attached group of people with a real sense of family belonging.

A CHILD OF DIVORCE

I myself had a glancing encounter with remarriage in my own life. My father was married four times. I am the daughter of his third marriage, and I have two older sisters and a younger brother (now deceased). My parents separated when I was in my early teens—a separation that was akin to a flight, engineered and overseen by my big sisters. They were in the act of rescuing my gentle, thoroughly disempowered mother from a tyrannical, sometimes downright frightening husband. I was kept in the dark about the breakup until the eleventh hour, literally the moment when I came home to see the family furniture being loaded on a van.

The series of changes that followed was dismaying. We moved to a rented apartment in a tacky, somewhat scary neighborhood, and I had to switch to a high school where I hadn't a single acquaintance, let alone a friend. It was a difficult, lonesome period of my life.

My parents eventually divorced, but several years later, they made a doomed effort at reconciliation and remarried. I was working my way through college at that time, and moved home for economic reasons. My older sisters were on their own by then (one was already married), so I was the sole witness present for the second marital dissolution.

Both my parents remarried later on in their lives. My father was in his late seventies when he took his fourth bride, Mira—a sweet-tempered woman like my mother (where did he find them?). I was married by then, and the mother of two of my three daughters; I didn't see the couple very often. But I do recall how taken aback I was on those occasions when Mira offered me "maternal" advice about how I should relate to my father with more daughterly warmth. I almost laughed in her face. What did this veritable stranger know about his atrocious track record as a nightmare husband and parent? I was civil to her but paid scant attention to her exhortations.

In my own adult life, I have always considered myself a child of divorce but never as a child of remarriage. I was too old when my parents married other partners, and I related to these new spouses in only the most superficial ways. So when I started my research on the topic of remarriage, I had a romanticized *Brady Bunch* view of the subject. I believed that the newly married couple and their children would come together and blend easily into a warm new family whole.

THE REMARRIAGE JOURNEY

Some thirteen years ago, as divorce and remarriage were becoming an ever more evident aspect of American life, I began delving into the subject. I had already written three successful works on relationships: one on women and depression, a second one on couples, and a third one on families. But to my surprise, there wasn't a great deal of useful research available on remarried life. There were a few books by distinguished clinicians, but they were not easy reading for a lay audience. Thus, I felt very fortunate when I came across a model of remarriage written by a then-graduate student, Patricia Papernow. It was called *The Remarriage Journey,* and it seemed to lay out my path very clearly.

Here, in abbreviated form, are the six stages of the journey Papernow outlines:

1. *Myth and fantasy*: A time of hope and high illusion, such as instant intimacy among all members of the newly reconstituted family.
2. *Bewilderment*: The fantasies come under siege and the realities (e.g., the oldest, strongest attachments are those shared by the biological parent and the children) make themselves felt.
3. *Awareness*: Members of the family begin creating a vocabulary for their experiences and put names to the feelings they are experiencing.
4. *Mobilization*: Changes start to happen. Whereas earlier the stepcouple kept their disappointments and distress under wraps, things now emerge in the open—often with a bang!
5. *Reorganization and restructuring*: This stage could be called "going into business together." The couple and their family members roll up their sleeves and get to work on negotiating and managing their differences.
6. *Resolution:* The remarried family's honeymoon period, a time when everyone settles into the new structure and becomes a truly integrated, operational unit in which *all* family members are included. The new family gains a real sense that this is "home"—that a new, mutually created family territory now exists.

With this succinct model in mind, I began a series of interviews with remarried mates. I wanted to learn as much as possible about the sorts of issues that confronted them and the families they had joined together. Prominent among my interview subjects were a number of couples belonging to a local stepfamily support group that met for discussions on a weekly basis. There were some twenty couples in the group, though attendance fluctuated; I also interviewed most of the partners in private settings (their homes or my office). I interviewed some of their remarried friends, too, as well as people who volunteered when I gave lectures. The model I was using seemed flawless at the outset; but as I came to know the couples, their unique stories, and the struggles they faced, the framework didn't seem to map clearly onto their real-life circumstances.

My plan of action had been to interview many remarried partners and eventually write at length about one couple at each stage of the journey. However, as these sessions continued, I realized that on closer scrutiny, the members of the pair often didn't seem to fit into the neat categories Papernow had outlined. On the contrary, the couples were all over the place, especially early on in the remarriage. One partner might be in the uncomfortable stage of awareness, while the other was still mired in the stage of myth and fantasy. One partner might be in lost in bewilderment, while the other was ready to move onward into the stage of reorganization and restructuring. On a number of occasions, there were individuals who seemed to be at more than one stage of the journey simultaneously, say, partly awareness and partly mobilization.

I could not write about these couples in a coherent manner, for the truth was that the members of the remarried pair were too often not in the same developmental stage. So it was that eventually—and with much chagrin and regret—I had to put this absorbing remarriage project on hold.

Would I ever return to it? I wasn't sure.

THE SOBERING STATISTICS

As the twentieth century moved into the twenty-first, sweeping changes in the demography of American family life were continuing apace. As sociologist Andrew Cherlin observes in his recent book *The Marriage-Go-Round,* "Both marriage and divorce contribute to the larger picture of a country [the United States] in which people partner, unpartner and repartner faster than they do in any other Western nation." When it comes to intimate partnerships, Americans seem to be on speed.

After a divorce, as Cherlin notes, ex-spouses in this country seem to find a new partner more quickly than happens in other nations. They often form cohabiting (living together) relationships easily, but also end them more swiftly. This story of fragile partnerships creates a situation of flux and uncertainty, especially for the children involved.

Precise statistics on marriage and remarriage in the United States are hard to come by. Some experts say the numbers of failed first marriages are in the 50 percent range, and some say that number, which tripled between 1960 and 1980, has stabilized and even dropped slightly.

As far as the statistics on remarriage (and cohabitation) are concerned, they are even more unclear, and they vary depending on the source. Certainly remarital failure is higher than in first marriages by at least 10 percent. However, that 60 percent figure is the lowest I have seen. Some experts and authors have suggested even higher numbers, such as 65 percent and 70 percent. This latter, somewhat improbable figure is the one Wednesday Martin uses in her smart, angry book *Stepmonsters,* which depicts the stepmother as the ultimate victim.

According to stepfamily researcher Larry Ganong, 40 percent of all new marriages now contain at least one partner who has been married before. And perhaps equally surprising is the result of a recent Pew Research Center survey: researchers found that at the current time, one in four Americans has a close steprelative. That is a quarter of the U.S. population!

In the decade-plus interval following my ill-starred effort to write about remarriage (during which I had written two new books, one on emotional trauma and the other on long-lasting marriages) there was a huge outburst of academic interest in the subject. Many recoupling studies were undertaken and yielded solid, practical findings.

Among the many questions studied were these: Does the stepparent ever have the right to punish the stepchild, or should the blood-related parent be the only one to do it? Is there a difference between what first-marriage couples and stepcouples fight most about? Will the newly formed family unify more quickly if they engage in many joint activities? When it comes to finances, what works best in terms of creating family warmth, trust, and empathy: the one-pot solution (couples pool their money), the two-pot solution (each remarried partner pays his or her own way and that of his or her children), or the three-pot solution (the partners keep separate accounts, but create a third kitty for household expenses)? An ever growing remarriage literature was providing reliable answers to these and a host of other questions.

The problem was that it wasn't being widely read—even by therapists whose practices included many reconstituted families. Indeed, in the years between 1997, when I had put aside my work on remarriage, and 2009, when I turned on the lights again, *no* clinician had written a book firmly based on this rapidly accumulating research evidence.

Also, curiously enough, the dynamics of remarriage and stepfamily life were rarely (almost never) taught in family therapy training courses. It was (and still is) generally assumed that if you have learned how to work therapeutically with first-marriage families, you can extend your clinical knowledge enough to deal with the issues of remarried parents and their children. But alas, nothing could be further from the truth.

THE ARCHITECTURAL MODEL
AS METAPHOR

As the academic studies of remarriage continued to multiply, a small but dedicated band of clinicians and researchers were paying close attention to the flow of results. Outstanding among them was Dr. Patricia Papernow, who was busily crafting an updated model—one that was not at variance with her remarriage journey metaphor but was far more focused on the here-and-now in terms of the major remarriage predicaments that might emerge and how to go about managing them. Very importantly, this new model was solidly based on *evidence*: the multiplicity of findings that the remarriage researchers had amassed.

Papernow called this new model the *architectural model* in order to underscore the idea that first-marriage families and remarried families can be likened to two discrete buildings whose basic blueprints differ significantly. Everyone is of course familiar with the layout of the first-marriage structure, but the design of the remarried family is relatively unknown. Few people even understand that it is constructed according to a fundamentally different design plan. This elemental difference is due to the crucial fact that biological parents have long-standing, deep connections to their blood- and heart-related children and newcomer/stepparents do not.

This situation sets up an array of crucial challenges, and a basic tenet of the architectural model is that remarrying partners will typically encounter several or all of them. Some of these challenges will be readily recognizable to those who have experienced them, but many remarried couples have never heard of any of them—although they may be dealing with them on a daily basis. Awareness of these common experiences, along with a clear language with which to discuss the problems that beset merging families, is an enormous boon for remarried partners struggling to deal with a host of unanticipated dilemmas.

Papernow's architectural model gave me a critical new perspective on the reality of the daily lives of the couples I'd focused on in my earlier research. It was easy to see why it had been impossible to fit them neatly into the stages associated with a journey. The process of integrating disparate family units is far more complex than a movement from point A to point B. The notion of planning, designing, and erecting a building that will suit the newly joined family is a much more apt metaphor.

Come to think of it, all architecture is about organizing human relationships in spatial terms. The first-marriage family structure can be erected without much thought, using what architects refer to as "the vernacular"; that is, conventional methods of planning. Picture a home with a central hallway, a living room on one side, a dining room and a kitchen on the other, and three bedrooms upstairs. No special architectural expertise is needed to construct this building. Metaphorically speaking, it corresponds to the first-marriage family—the family most of us grew up in. It is the family that exists in our heads, and we know how to go about building it.

A remarried family, on the other hand, presents a number of design challenges. The replacement of a missing mate (due to divorce, desertion, or death) does not restore the family to its first-marriage status. On the contrary, it presents a number of complex design issues that require the new family to discard what architects refer to as "conventional planning." The remarried couple and their children must leave behind many of their old assumptions about how a family structure is supposed to look and get to work on self-consciously creating a diagram and then planning, designing, and building an entirely new kind of edifice that will realistically meet their particular needs.

This is where the notion of architectural expertise comes in. The new family consists of people who are coming together when they are older, and one or both may have children by former relationships. Since the family they build together will differ fundamentally from the more traditional first-marriage family design, their automatic assumptions about family organization must be dismantled, reanalyzed, and reconfigured in ways that will suit their newly amalgamating group. The architectural model does this: it suggests practical ways in which to meet the special difficulties inherent in later marriages—specific know-how that can help the members of the family interact and integrate comfortably. It also helps the new family in the creation of their own unique (nurturing but *different* from a first-marriage design layout) remarriage blueprint.

It was Papernow's new model, plus the meteoric growth of remarriage itself, that galvanized me into action after having let my research on this topic lay fallow for so many years. Her crisp definition of the challenges faced by remarrying partners clarified my understanding of so much of what I had seen and heard but not yet fully understood when first interviewing the couples—and it made me realize why the "journey" framework had proven too abstract and insufficient.

THE FIVE STRUCTURAL CHALLENGES OF REMARRIAGE

A basic tenet of the architectural model is that there are five major challenges faced by remarrying partners, and they will typically encounter several or all of them. Some of these challenges will be readily recognizable by the reader, but many remarrying partners have never heard of any of them.

The Powerful Impact of Insider/Outsider Forces

Insider/outsider forces are a basic, inbuilt feature of remarriage. They tend to shift the members of the couple into opposite positions because their early experiences of the marriage are so different. One partner (the outsider) often feels left out and rejected when the mate's children are on the scene. The other partner (the insider) feels wrenched between his or her lifelong commitment to his or her offspring and the person he or she has fallen in love with and married.

In brief, the insider parent is trying hard to mediate between the way the family used to operate and the different ways the outsider partner feels it should operate in the future. To be noted is the fact that in families where both mates bring children to the marriage, these insider/outsider roles can switch around depending on whose youngsters are on the scene.

The Children Involved Have Undergone Early Losses
and Hard Transitions

Children experience the initial loss of the intact family—be it due to divorce (95 percent are) or death—as a volcanic upheaval, inevitably bringing deep grief and fears of abandonment in its wake. A striking example of a child's bitterness and sorrow appears in chapter 4, my interviews with the Jamisons. Abbie Jamison's son, Rob, became upset and rejecting toward both his mother and stepdad when Abbie's remarriage required a move clear across the country and a separation from the boy's loving grandparents, cousins, school, and friends.

Furthermore, the subsequent marriage is very likely to arouse a conflict of loyalties. The children of remarriage are often assailed by the guilty feeling that harboring liking —or even outright loving—feelings for the "replacement parent" is a betrayal of the "real," biological parent (in reality or in memory if that parent has died).

Parenting Tasks Tend to Move the Partners into Intense and Opposing Positions

This challenge tends to move the partners into hotly contested, oppositional positions. The stepparent wants to effect some changes in the way the mate's single-parent family system has hitherto operated—for over time, families with this type of structure tend to become too lax and permissive. However, the stepchildren ignore or defy his or her requests; they've suffered through too many demands for change already and want things to remain just as they were before the stranger/stepparent entered the scene. The natural parent wants both to please his or her new spouse and yet reassure the children that things will stay the same and they won't experience any more earth-shaking transitions.

It is true that during the period of singlehood, the biological parent's authority has slipped a bit, and he or she is likely to be overly permissive. So while the stepparent wants to demand more order and respectfulness, the natural parent wants to cut the children an unusual amount of slack and excuses many of their questionable behaviors.

This issue emerged most visibly in my interviews with Julie and Matthew Albright, described in chapter 1. Julie wanted to set limits on her stepson, Gabe, during the times when he was in her care. Matthew and his ex-wife, Fran, overruled her, thereby depriving her of authority as the female head of her household.

Uniting Two Disparate Family Cultures

The vast challenge presented here involves the plenitude of differences that each party brings to the newly created stepfamily. Agreement on everything from whether you can start eating before everyone sits down at the table to whether you hang your coat on a hook or throw it on the sofa are simply taken for granted by the biological parent and the children but are unknown and often not understood by the newest member of the family.

The difficulties that emerge in this situation have to do with the relatively thin common ground (implicit knowledge of habits, rules, routines) shared by the remarried partners and the thick common ground forged over years by the biological parent and his or her offspring. A new common ground must be created over the course of time, one that will be satisfying and comfortable for all members of the newly created family system.

A good example of this particular challenge appears in chapter 6, the tale of the Burkes, where new wife Carole was incensed by Ted's adult children's refusal to clean up the kitchen in the ways that meant a lot to her. The fact that these small requests were being routinely ignored made her feel invisible and as if she might be "going crazy." She felt like an alien, as if she didn't belong in Ted's family's household.

Also, in chapter 8, I recount the tale of the Perez/de Matteo couple and describe the clashes that can occur when two different family cultures and two different ethnic cultures exist simultaneously. In regard to this latter couple, it should be noted that some 50 percent of Americans presently marry outside their own ethnic group, and the rate of socioeconomic and cultural intermarriage climbs even higher in remarriage situations.

As shown in chapter 8, Vicki de Matteo and Miguel Perez were communicating with one another through not one but two sets of misunderstandings.

Extension of Family Boundaries

In a first-marriage nuclear family, the members include the biological parents and their blood-related (or adopted) dependent children. In the case of remarriage, the new household will not be complete as it stands, for there will be a family member living outside it (the other biological parent) who must be included within the overall system. Therefore, there will be a "boundary with a hole in it" to offer this parent easy access.

As we shall see with the Duvaliers in chapter 3, this unclosed boundary can be fraught with difficulties. Cliff's first wife had eloped with his close friend, basically leaving him to mourn for her eternally (she believed). Thus, his enormous contentment with second wife Sara seemed to irk the first wife tremendously, and she was doing everything possible to upset the remarried couple by interfering in their lives whenever and wherever she could.

MANAGING THE FIVE CHALLENGES

When it comes to meeting the five major challenges, the notion of a remarriage structure comes in handy once again. This imaginary edifice should be pictured as existing on three levels. The top level would consist of the five challenges described above. As Papernow told me in the course of our frequent conversations, many remarried couples need no more than a clear understanding of these challenges and the language with which to discuss and negotiate about them. She calls this first pass at managing the challenges *psychoeducation*.

On the level below, Papernow lays out a second and allied approach to remarriage issues, which she calls *interpersonal skills.* This level of understanding has to do with how the partners address each other on particularly sensitive issues—especially parenting, which is among the most sensitive of all remarriage concerns. A simple example is the use of "I" messages: thus, instead of saying, "Your bratty kids come in and walk right past me without saying hello," a stepparent might phrase her distress as, "It really hurts my feelings when your children run in and hug and kiss you and ignore my presence completely." The second approach is more likely to start a sympathetic discussion rather than a fight.

At the lowest, deepest level of the remarriage building are what Papernow calls *psychic bruises in bad places.* These refer to painful, unresolved issues dating back to a person's life in his or her family of origin. Certainly such issues can and frequently do make their appearance in first-marriage relationships as well; but in remarriage situations they can have a particular poignancy. For instance, if a person was unable to please people in his or her family of origin, feeling unwelcome in this new family environment can be a particularly difficult blow to sustain. Or if a stepparent felt ignored and discounted during childhood, remarried family situations are highly likely to exacerbate old wounds when members of the biologically related group go about their accustomed business and simply disregard his or her wishes and requests. In chapter 5, which concerns the Meyers, we see the phenomenal impact that Greg's parents' tormented marriage had upon his subsequent life: two failed marriages were behind him when he finally *got it right* and connected with the warm and empathic Caroline.

THE GREAT UNSPOKEN

Money is often a remarkably taboo subject of discussion among remarrying couples. The partners may talk over their former sexual and marital histories at length but avoid the topic of their financial histories and current economic state completely. A request to look over the partner's spreadsheet would sound so invasive, so unromantic! And yet remarriage involves a complex array of money issues that need to be clearly understood and dealt with—matters such as life insurance, pensions, upcoming college tuitions, legal home ownership, and outstanding unpaid debts are just some among them. Furthermore, people come to later marriages with relatively fixed "money personalities"; for instance, some pay their bills as soon as they arrive, while others throw them in a drawer until some more auspicious moment or don't object to not paying them until they're well past due.

In chapter 7, "Wedding Bells and Dollar Bills," I present a compendium of the financial information with which anyone contemplating remarriage should be well acquainted. I also suggest a few ingenious ways to start a conversation on the subject of finances without giving offense to the presumptive or newly re-wed partner. A chilling caveat emptor appears in chapter 6, "Boundless Trust," my interviews with the Burkes. Their story presents a stark illustration of what can go wrong when the financial status and spending habits of a new mate remain vague and poorly understood.

SOMETHING OLD, SOMETHING NEW

The Remarriage Blueprint is in part a longitudinal study. In the course of my more recent research, I revisited a group of couples I had first spoken with during my first round of interviews some twelve years earlier. Since then, the research on remarriage—and the rate of repartnering in general—had grown so dramatically that I decided to return and reinterview a number of the couples whom I had first seen in my initial 1997–98 sample.

This didn't prove easy, for many of these pairs had moved on. They had scattered to different neighborhoods or different areas of the country without leaving any forwarding information. I wondered about them but had no knowledge of how their remarriages had fared during the past twelve-plus years. Fortunately, though, I did manage to reconnect with a number of engaging couples. In these pages, I tell the stories of two of those marriages as they played out over time because they are vivid illustrations of some important points that need to be made. The other remarried pairs whose stories appear in these pages were first interviewed more recently, between 2009 and 2011, when this interviewer had much more research data in hand and a far more focused and useful model of remarriage available.

CHAPTER ONE

The Myth of Instant Love: Julie and Matthew Albright, 1997 and 2009

THE ALBRIGHTS IN 1997

Julie and Matthew Albright were among the first group of volunteers for my research on remarriage. I interviewed them in the late 1990s and then reinterviewed them some twelve years later. When I first met them, they had been married for a long time— eight years —yet an electric sense of this pair's passionate, highly charged involvement was evident from the very outset. In fact I found myself checking and rechecking the wedding date I'd jotted down, because the two of them focused on each other with so much intensity that their relationship seemed more like a sexy, supercharged, very new one.

This was a third marriage for Julie, age forty-five, and a second one for Matthew, who was seven years older. Having celebrated their eighth anniversary shortly before I interviewed them in 1997, the Albrights had already been married for three years beyond what is deemed the five-year danger zone for remarried partners. They seemed secure in their connection, and my impression was that they were still very much in love. Still, in the course of our meetings, I became aware that they were clearly struggling with a number of issues, especially ones involving their vastly different styles of parenting.

Julie had had a daughter when she was twenty, in her first marriage, who was seventeen years old by the time she and Matthew married. Matthew had first been married at age twenty-five, and his only child, Gabe, was born when he was thirty-seven. He and his first wife had separated and divorced two years later.

In Matthew's view, the fact that when they married, Julie's daughter, Leslie, was about to leave for college was "nothing short of a godsend. Julie's daughter took off pretty soon after we got married, and thank the Lord, because Leslie was a horror," Matthew said, in a curt, dismissive voice. "Talk about horrors . . . absolutely."

Taken aback by the force of these words, my gaze shifted to Julie quickly. Her wide gray eyes had grown even wider and her slender body seemed to stiffen, but her neutral expression hadn't changed. She ran a hand through her soft, brown, curly hair but said nothing.

Then Matthew said more pacifically, "Of course, at that time, I'd had no experience with adolescents—my son, Gabe, was then seven, and now he's fifteen, so I know what it's like to have an adolescent horror around." He chuckled, the amused laugh of a proud, indulgent father.

Then he went on. "But Julie's daughter was awful, just awful—very needy and very competitive with her mom. Unfortunately, she can't begin to compete with her mom where looks and physical attractiveness are concerned." I glanced at Julie, thinking, *Yes, she is beautiful.* "And my God"—Matthew's voice was rising—"Leslie was so temperamental, the most self-centered person! You had to be a real parent to love this kid."

He hesitated, was met with silence, and then his voice took on an even more offended tone: "She just didn't have much regard for others; she would walk down the stairs and wouldn't say 'good morning,' and basically was prone to exhibiting what I would call antisocial behavior. Leslie could really bring a cloud into a room."

Matthew Albright, who is a very tall, large, well-built man with wavy salt-and-pepper hair, leaned forward in his chair and looked fixedly at his wife. I had the passing thought that his size felt slightly intimidating. Julie hadn't spoken, simply shaken her head in disagreement.

I paused, took a breath, and then asked her straightforwardly if she'd felt let down by the negative ways in which her spouse had reacted to her daughter's adolescent antics. A pained expression crossed her face. "I felt then," she said, "and still do feel disappointed by how much criticism he's given me about the way in which I brought my daughter up. He's been endlessly critical about the parenting job that I've done."

She gazed at me fixedly, as if excluding Matthew from the conversation. "I myself think the way we parent is just different. Leslie and I have a very close relationship—we're two *girls*. I was a young mother. Matthew grew up in a house with a brother and a father, and eventually he had a son. Then he gets me in a house, and I have a daughter—and girls treat each other very differently. They can get very explosive, and then a second later it's as if it never happened. And it's true, Leslie did wear her mood on her face and was very needy. At the same time, she was on the brink of leaving home just as Mommy was moving in with this wealthy Prince Charming, and Mommy was living in a big, beautiful new house with a little seven-year-old boy who was going to get all of Mommy's attention." My gaze drifted to the enormous diamond on Julie's left ring finger. "And now my daughter was leaving for school. . . . I think Leslie was in a very tough spot."

Out of Sync

I reflected that Julie's daughter had indeed been in a tough situation. In terms of the family life cycle, Leslie's task was to establish emotional bonds with her newly acquired family members; at the same time, in terms of her individual life cycle, she was in the process of her normal adolescent leave-taking.

Complexities of this sort are not uncommon in remarrying families, where a particular member's life-cycle issue (in Leslie's case, that of leaving home) and the task of establishing connections with the newly forming family may be confusingly out of sync. So, it should be said, may be the differing family life-cycle experiences of the new spouses. Julie Albright was the parent of an almost mature daughter, and Matthew Albright had never parented either a daughter or a teenager. As the father of a seven-year-old son, he'd had neither patience nor sympathy for his stepdaughter and no concept of what adolescents—particularly female adolescents—are typically all about.

The Myth of Instant Love

Let me pause here and address the subject of fantasy. I don't think of fantasies in pejorative terms; my own thoughts run along the opposite lines. Idealizing, hopeful fantasies are wonderful, and wonderfully normal, and we all bring them into newly developing relationships. However, it is crucial to recognize the special character of the rose-tinted fantasies that many couples carry into remarriage. These highly positive expectations are fueled by powerful hopes of repairing the family system that was torn asunder, whether by divorce or death. And the most pervasive fantasy of all is the myth of instant love. This is the new couple's belief that they and the children of their former relationships will combine easily into a loving, joyous family group.

At the time of his second marriage, Matthew Albright had clearly been swept up into this most potent of all remarriage fantasies: he'd believed that his new wife and his young son would blend together instantly and without difficulty in a mutually tender and loving relationship.

He now told me, in a voice tinged with anger, that he had entered this marriage fully confident that his happiness with Julie would enable them to quickly create the kind of active, harmonious family life that he had always wanted. This would happen with special ease because her teenage daughter, Leslie, was leaving for college, and his own easygoing young son would be with them on a joint-custody, every-other-week basis.

"Gabe was just seven years old when we got married—a gorgeous, smart, happy little kid. Who would *not* love this kid?" he demanded. "I didn't even give it a second thought, Julie moving into this house and just loving every moment of being with this boy. He was a little angel, and he was my son, and *she* loved *me*, and so it was all going to be perfect. I had an image of us all coming together sort of like the Brady Bunch—that we would share a lot of interests, do lots of things together.

"So a lot of strong expectations were driving my behavior, and I was probably pretty awful in terms of what I did to Julie—manipulating her relationship with Gabe and wanting it to be a certain way. It got pretty tense; it got so that if Julie walked into the house and my boy was there, and she didn't hug him and give him a big kiss and a big hello, I just felt terrible. It would get me so upset because I wanted to make things right. I wanted it to be *perfect,* and I know I put a lot of pressure on her.

"But at the same time, issues about Gabe kept coming up and creating a lot of strain and arguments. We were on pretty shaky ground, and I began feeling that she doesn't want my kid to be around us, that he is going to be a bother to her! This didn't go down very well with me, who has the perfect child. Who would *not* want the perfect child?" He sounded baffled, hurt, and belligerent.

It was a rhetorical question, one that didn't require a response—and I was glad that one was not expected. As an interviewer whose main job is to be a listener, I refrained from pointing out to Matthew that while he was openly contemptuous of Julie's daughter, he'd expected his wife to love his "perfect" son instantly and unconditionally. But nothing had proceeded as he'd expected.

"The things that started happening hit me hard at the time," Matthew recounted, "and I guess I did feel fairly blindsided. Because in so many ways we did, as a couple, have everything going for us. I care very deeply about Julie, and because of my love for her, I started out with the expectation that it was just going to work out effortlessly, that there wouldn't be any problems at all." He paused, and added flatly, "Things came to a pass where they were getting really bitter, and we were no more than a hair's breadth away from splitting up."

I glanced at Julie, who seemed to be cowering in her chair and wore a frightened expression on her face.

This father's fantasy had been that his new bride, because of her love for him, would naturally adore his young child from the first instant—even before she'd had time to form any kind of relationship with the boy. This irrational sort of belief, one that is rampant among remarrying partners, was that she-who-loves-you will automatically love your child or children with a fervor and intensity equal to your own. Not only will your new mate love your children, but your children will blossom under the warmth of this wonderful parental stand-in's affection and will return the affection fully. Simply by virtue of being brought together, all of the step-relatives will become fully engaged, loving intimates on the spot.

But it is unreasonable to suppose that all of the people in a remarried family are going to love or even like one another; after all, it is the adults who have fallen in love, not the children. What has been papered over by this comforting myth is the simple truth that human relationships take time to grow and cannot be simply foisted on people. After all, the newcomer is going to take up what was previously their own time and space.

Moreover, the attempt to force love and affection creates a negative dynamic that usually leads to just the opposite situation. A certain period of adaptation—time in which to work out those mutually satisfactory roles, rules, and rhythms of being that are the new family's common ground—is required as the members of the group get to know the relative strangers with whom they have found themselves living.

She Who Loves Me Must Adore My Son

Matthew Albright had taken it as a moral given that the woman who loved him must naturally adore his child with an intensity equal to his own. When she'd failed to do so—or to do so with the expected amount of enthusiasm—Matthew was rocked by frustration and disappointment. Soon he'd begun blaming her for not being the devotedly maternal partner he'd expected her to be. To some degree, he felt as if Julie had misled and betrayed him.

However, she had fallen in love with the father, not with the child. Realistically speaking, forging an authentic, loving connection to Matthew's son would require some familiarizing time, a degree of patience, and the cumulative effect of many small daily experiences. But before any of these good things could happen, before sufficient common ground could be established, she'd been placed in the highly paradoxical position of being commanded to love Gabe spontaneously.

It is hard to imagine showering heartfelt hugs and kisses on a child when someone else has legislated those hugs beforehand. Julie's failure to respond to Gabe in the ways her new husband presumed she ought to had begun making her feel increasingly guilty, inadequate, and deeply misunderstood. Inevitably, the boy had become a running issue between them, and Julie was feeling as unappreciated, hurt, and confused as her spouse.

A Husband and Two Wives

According to Julie, Matthew Albright had come into her life "like a real whirlwind." When the pair first encountered each other at the home of a mutual friend, she'd been a divorced single mother, grieving over not only the breakup of a second marriage but the loss of her beloved father.

"We met, and four days later Matthew, who has a financial consulting business, left for Kuwait on business. But then he called me three or four times from Kuwait! It all felt like something out of the movies—the romantic part," she related, her voice rising in excitement. "At the time, he used to drive a big white car, and it really did feel to me as if here was this big, huge, handsome guy who was going to come in on a white charger and carry me away. Take me away from all my troubles."

She laughed as if at her own naiveté, but then said seriously, "To a great degree, that's what he did do. Matthew is very much available to me in every way, very interested in who I am and what I do. How I deal with my daughter, who was almost seventeen when we got married. How I deal with his son. How I run my office. What clothes I wear. When we had sex last, or what did I like about the sex, or what didn't I like? Why don't we try it another way? He's always very complimentary about my body, about wanting to be with me, wanting to cuddle. He shops with me, buys me things: jewelry, earrings . . . anything. He takes an absolutely excessive interest in who I am and what I do. And sometimes it's impossible, but much of the time it's extraordinary."

She laughed again, looking simultaneously pleased and vaguely uneasy. I waited for her to continue, wondering at the same time how comfortable she actually found being monitored so carefully in this way.

In the brief silence that followed, I gazed outward through a row of seaward-facing glass windows. The Albrights' house is situated on a promontory overlooking Long Island Sound, and I watched a couple of anchored sailboats bobbing in the distance. Turning back, I glanced at Matthew Albright and, to my surprise, found him staring at his wife with a wary, somewhat skeptical expression.

"But still, for me, the tension level is high around here," said Julie, again focusing squarely on me and avoiding Matthew's eye. "I know it's high for him too, and I wish—" She left the sentence incomplete, drew in a long breath, then exhaled.

She began again. "I'm just feeling more and more of a need to have things calmer and easier," she said, her voice as subdued and guilty-sounding as if she were confessing to a misdeed. "We fight a lot, and it seems to me that most of the major disputes—which never really get resolved—are about parenting. I haven't ever felt validated parenting Matthew's son because I was told very early on that Gabe had a mom already. He has a very involved and active mom who lives not too far away."

In my initial work on the couple's family history, I'd learned that despite the breakup of Matthew and his ex-spouse, Fran's, marriage, she was still co-partner in their small but very successful consulting firm and continued to work closely with him. The two of them even traveled together from time to time, Julie told me, and both of them started laughing when they saw the surprised look on my face. She and Fran were good friends, she told me.

"Where is it written that you have to have a dreadful relationship—or no relationship—with your husband's ex-wife?" Julie asked, tilting her head to one side impishly. She felt quite comfortable about having Fran in their lives, she added, with a shrug. While she knew that many people found their situation strange, she valued her close friendship with Fran and considered her to be a rare and fine human being. There seemed to be no jealousies of a sexual nature dividing the two women—current wife and ex-wife—in Matthew's life. All of them had even vacationed together, Julie told me.

I said nothing. I was thinking of a book I'd been reading recently that contained a discussion about women who are divorced and yet keep clinging to the dead marital relationship. "Though the love is unrequited," author/psychotherapist Sandra Kahn writes, "and the man has moved on to a new love, loving him is known territory. In this feeling the [former spouse] finds a sense of history, a past that makes sense of the present." By not quitting the scene, she doesn't allow the old marriage fully to end or the remarriage fully to get started. A clear border between the old and new relationships is never established.

"Of course the point is that Matthew—" Julie resumed, then halted in midsentence. She started over: "Essentially, in many ways, Matthew has two wives." She sighed. "I wish that Fran, for her sake, could meet somebody, because I feel bad for her . . . and if that did happen, I think it would change the dynamics between all of us dramatically."

Matthew was frowning speculatively. "What do you think about that?" I asked him.

Not replying, he locked eyes with his wife, who went on, "Fran would have a main man in her life. Which would not be you."

"Yes," said Matthew.

"Which to a certain extent you still are," Julie continued.

Her husband stared at her with animus, "I think a lot of the crap would disappear," he said shortly. "The rivalry and jealousy and doubt and suspicion. It's almost a challenge to me, the way you put it! But personally, I would love to see that happen!"

This didn't sound like the happy threesome that Julie had described earlier. The boundary between Matthew Albright's former marriage and his present marriage was certainly a vague, indistinct one. Yet drawing a clear demarcation between the past relationship and the current one is among the essential tasks of a remarried couple, and in the Albrights' case, that boundary seemed to be almost nonexistent. Divorced parents remaining on good terms is one thing—and important to the child's well-being—but in this instance it seemed evident that a covert competition was very much in play when it came to parenting the original couple's son. Also, other barely submerged issues were arousing the "rivalry and jealousy and doubt and suspicion" that Matthew had referred to. Indeed, Julie gave me the impression that she felt as if she occupied the uneasy position of second wife in an emotionally polygamous marriage, one in which the first wife maintained an inordinate amount of power.

An Amorphous Kind of Being

The parenting of Gabe was *the* corrosive issue in the Albrights' current relationship, one to which the couple's conversation kept returning. Although Matthew spoke so contemptuously of her daughter, Julie had been expected to love her stepson from the outset. "At the same time I was let to know that I was not to be a parent. Period," stated Julie, bleakly. "Except that we had custody of Gabe every other week for the entire week, and often his dad was out of town traveling, sometimes with his ex-wife. Still, the understanding was that Matthew was the parent, and Fran was the parent, and I was . . . I don't know, an amorphous kind of being. At the same time, my behavior was under terrific scrutiny, so if I ever did anything discipline-wise or said something to this child about not talking back to me, I was ridiculed, criticized like crazy.

"But I just think it's self-contradictory to be told 'I want you to love my child,' and at the same time to be told, 'I don't want you to be that invested.' It means I have to watch every word that comes out of my mouth—I can't be spontaneous. Anyhow, that's how I feel. *Outside.* I just never could find my way *in there.*" She paused, looked at her husband nervously, and giggled as if to take the bite out of the things she'd been saying.

I said nothing, but my thought was that eight years into this passionate, loving marriage, a core challenge of remarriage—insider/outsider issues—was making itself felt very keenly.

Julie then looked at me, rolled her eyes, and said, "Uh-oh, he's making a lot of sounds, do you hear? We're going to get in a fight *right now.*"

I turned, saw that Matthew was leaning forward in his chair, and the expression on his face was ominous. "I'm going to say something now—I'm going to take a risk, here," he said. "To make a point, a tough point." He did look angry. How and when had that happened?

"Oh no, don't do that," said Julie lightly.

I laughed nervously, feeling surprised and off balance. It seemed to me that we'd moved from a fairly calm mood to one of hot anger without a transitional eyeblink. The conversation could be heading toward what psychotherapists call "a runaway"—a situation in which the interaction suddenly takes on a noxious urgency and threatens to go completely out of anyone's control.

I caught Matthew's eye, smiled, and said as peaceably as I could, "Do you want to respond to what Julie's been saying, Matthew? Because you *are* making little noises, and I think I see puffs of smoke coming out of your ears."

To my relief, he smiled back politely. But then he reiterated grimly, "I'll take a risk."

"Don't *do* that!" repeated Julie, laughing her high-pitched, apprehensive laugh again. As if to soothe herself, she began running her hand through her short, curly hair. This was followed by a long, tense silence, and then Matthew, to my relief, sat back in his chair and said nothing further.

Eight years into their marriage, the Albrights were clearly a couple who cared deeply for one another. In the course of our interviews, they told me that they were unshakably committed to this marriage. Whatever happened, they would never part. Nevertheless, it was also clear that some of their major challenges remained unresolved—and as Julie had said so forlornly, the level of conflict in the relationship was high.

"By definition, this has to be a very heedful, attentive relationship," Matthew observed thoughtfully at one point. "This isn't a situation you can simply glide through." Nevertheless, instead of negotiating and devising plans together around such unsettled issues as the parenting of Gabe and the unclear boundary between Matthew's first marriage and this current one, the Albrights were charging forward without any understanding of or empathy for the other's torn and painful position.

Insider/Outsider Dilemmas

It was easy to feel compassion for Julie, who had been placed in such an impotent position. She was expected to care for Gabe for long stretches of time during his dad's absences, yet to do so without any parental or even a babysitter's authority to enforce the (seemingly nonexistent) rules of her own home. She was firmly excluded from the blood-related system consisting of Matthew, his ex-wife, and their son.

Less evident was the terrible dilemma of the emotional insider, whose powerful fantasy of the loving new family had been shattered. Matthew had been convinced that Julie would adore his "perfect son" from the first instant and that the family they created together would be so filled with happiness that the lingering pain of the previous divorce would be healed. Instead he'd found himself trying desperately to satisfy the disparate needs of his second wife, his "angelic" son, and the ex-wife he still respected and cared about.

Having been the one to end his first marriage because it was, he said, "sexually dead," Matthew still remained ambivalent about the nature of his relationship with Fran. He often seemed uncertain whether his feelings toward his former spouse, who was still a major player in his life, were those of tenderness or of unresolved guilt. It seemed evident that he'd never been able to leave that failed marriage completely behind him, and his ex-wife had really never let him do so.

"Actually, Fran called up last Sunday and said she wanted to wish me a happy anniversary," Matthew said, at the end of our first round of interviews. "I asked her what she was talking about, and she said, 'It's *today*. Aren't you going to wish me something?' And I said, no, I knew that her birthday was on Tuesday. She said, 'Yes, that's right,' and reminded me that we had met two days before her birthday twenty-four years earlier. And then she told me that she wanted to call me up and tell me that I've known her for a whole half of her lifetime. She said, 'I want you to know that in spite of everything that's happened—all that's gone on—how much I care about you. How much I still love you and cherish our relationship.'"

"She also said, 'and how happy I am,'" appended Julie drily.

"Yes, 'how happy I am and how good my life is.' That's it," said Matthew, looking confused and full of self-reproach. After eight years of marriage to Julie, he remained transfixed by what some experts have termed the "biological force-field." He was trying to forge a fresh relationship with a different wife but was still torn between the legitimate needs of this second marriage and the strong pull of the first-family biological system.

THE ALBRIGHTS IN 2009

It was in the spring of 2009, twelve years after our initial set of interviews, that I got in touch with Julie Albright to ask if she and Matthew would be willing to participate in a few follow-up conversations. I was in for some unexpected news: Julie hesitated for a long moment and then said that they had divorced a couple of years ago after an eighteen-year marriage.

Julie's voice on the telephone sounded hushed, almost spooked. She said she felt pretty raw and that the breakup still felt unreal to her. Nevertheless, she would very much like to talk with me. Matthew was now living abroad, but he would be returning to the States for a brief stay in the near future. She could say with certainty that he would be willing to be interviewed too.

We met in my home office in Hamden, Connecticut. Before Julie arrived, I read through our long-ago interviews and was particularly struck by both partners' assertions that they were unshakably committed to this marriage—that whatever happened, they would never part. I also remembered how much I'd liked them as a couple. There had been such an aura of passion and excitement about them. Despite their obvious difficulties, I'd believed that those strong, positive feelings would ultimately enable them to construct a more integrated, far less combative family environment.

It was a Saturday afternoon, and when Julie arrived, she was dressed casually, almost carelessly, in a pair of slim jeans and a pale blue sweater with a small moth hole on one sleeve. She wore her softly curling hair, now laced with strands of gray, in a fluffy ponytail. I learned that she was now working as a psychological counselor in a renowned private high school in suburban Connecticut. She owned her own home in Westport; it had been part of the financial settlement.

"So," I began, leaning forward to switch on the recorder that sat on a low table between us. "Tell me what happened."

"Tell you what happened?" she asked me, her dark eyes widening as if I'd made the most astonishing request. She didn't reply. She simply stared at me, as if bewildered.

I decided to back up and ask her about what had taken place

in the couple's relationship during the long interval since I had last seen them. I smiled and said, "You seemed like a pretty sexy couple at that time."

"We seemed sexy?" she asked, then answered her own question. "Absolutely, we were. When we met, we connected immediately on a visceral level. It was a blind date, and when Matthew walked in, it was just like fireworks. I just fell for him, and he fell for me—or seemed to. Yes, he was a highly sexual person, and I was a highly sexual-looking person—but basically I had many inhibitions."

At that time, Julie said, she was still recovering from a second marriage that had come to a traumatic conclusion due to a lifeless sexual relationship. Her second husband had almost never wanted sex; Matthew, on the other hand, wanted sex all the time. "Don't forget that he traveled a lot, but when he was at home, we had sex every day. For me, that was too much, but I had no voice. I was so mesmerized by him. I thought he was so beautiful and so powerful. And most of the time, he treated me like a princess."

She smiled ruefully and said that she had gone from being active in the women's movement to becoming a little doll who was being showered with designer clothes, jewelry, expensive perfumes, and exotic vacations. "Matthew lived in this extraordinary world that was powered by tons of money, and I became a kind of co-conspirator. I surrendered myself to it completely."

However, they fought throughout the marriage. "We were always fighting and having sex," said Julie with a sad little shrug of her shoulders.

As their years together went on and the physical symptoms of her menopause became manifest, their sexual relationship—the core factor of their bond—became a source of conflict. "I had vaginal dryness, and sex was painful. At the same time, Matthew started having trouble with erections. Of course he was on a lot of different medications, and what I now know—but didn't then—is that these can induce performance problems. But he blamed me. He said that his erection problems were happening because I wasn't interested."

During that arc of time, they had moved from the large, glass-windowed house by the sea that Matthew had built just before meeting Julie. In his own mind, she now reflected, that home had been a symbol of his success and a place in which he would have liked to live forever. But she had felt chilly all the time there, and when Gabe left for boarding school at age four-teen, she had been alone during Matthew's frequent travels.

"Also, the house was built for someone who was six feet four, and I am five feet three. This meant I couldn't reach the cabinets or sit on the toilets without my feet up in the air. So, finally, we bought a lovely old home in Westport, and I adored it. But Matthew was so deeply angry about having lost his big showpiece that I think he never forgave me. Moving away from that house was something he felt as an injury. It just wounded him terribly," said Julie, her voice contrite.

Another problem from the very outset, she said, had been Matthew's son, Gabe. There had been tension in the room whenever the three of them were present. "Gabe became, very quickly, the insurmountable obstacle to any intimacy in our marriage. I was expected to worship this kid but not to have any authority over him or opinions about his behavior. I think Matthew faulted me a lot for what he called 'the climate' in the house whenever his son was around. We never became the family he'd expected us to become, and I know he was bitterly disappointed.

"The other thing I would say is that Matthew never protected me. He never had my back—not with Gabe, not with his ex-wife, not with anybody. Even if I got into a disagreement with a friend, he never took my side. Never," Julie repeated. "Never."

What had made the marriage finally break apart? I returned to my original question.

Julie was now ready to respond. She said quietly, "We broke up in January of 2006. We'd gone to Paris for my fifty-fourth birthday. It was Matthew, Gabe, my daughter, my son-in-law, and me. And what happened while we were there—it was a bizarre story. During that vacation, Matthew essentially became a different person. I can't even go into that—I feel so terrible about what happened in the marriage."

Her face clouded over, and she stopped speaking. I said nothing, simply looked at her sympathetically and waited.

When Julie resumed speaking, it was in disorganized snatches of information. "He had turned sixty-one two weeks before my birthday. We were both feeling on the edge of the cliff. And on the plane trip to Paris, we talked about maybe having to separate. But when we got there, he seemed to flip out—literally—and become a different person. He changed his whole wardrobe into an avant-garde, bohemian style. He bought this very expensive little mid-cap and ragged jeans and gold chains."

I couldn't repress a smile. "In other words, a teenage outfit," I said.

Julie returned the smile, shook her head as if to say she knew that for a man in his sixties this behavior was absurd. "Totally teenage," she said, "and he began staying out in bars until three a.m. or sometimes four a.m. By himself, or sometimes his son joined him."

I asked how old Gabe was at that point, and Julie said that he was twenty-three. "When my birthday arrived, Matthew basically didn't even acknowledge it. Didn't buy me anything, not even a hankie. It was as if he was in Paris all by himself. When he wasn't sitting in bars, he was in Starbucks on his computer, negotiating business. Then there were the phone calls. He was making them all the time."

I nodded as if to say that I understood: Matthew had zoned out, begun acting as if she weren't present. At the same time, I was recalling how Julie had once said that Matthew took an almost excessive interest in everything about her, that he shopped with her, bought her "jewelry, earrings, perfume, everything." On that birthday visit, he was making his total disinterest apparent.

To my surprise, Julie now said that even though she'd started out on that trip feeling infuriated with Matthew and contemplating separation, she'd been convinced that she was going to have a good time.

Good time? I thought incredulously, and as if she'd been reading my thoughts, she went on to say, "We'd rented a beautiful apartment with a lovely view. The kids—my daughter and her husband—were there. We went to museums, we did everything. But it was so weird. Knowing Matthew as little as you do, you must remember: He would fall over himself making surprises for me and buying me things to the point where it was ridiculous. Then, just as ridiculous, he flipped the other way."

She stopped, looking as if the very recollection had stunned her. I asked her if Matthew had accompanied her on the museum trips and sightseeing, and she shook her head to say that he hadn't. Neither had Gabe, who'd been distant and inert much of the time and who'd simply hung around the apartment doing nothing.

It was in the immediate aftermath of that trip that she and Matthew had separated, and it had actually occurred while she was sleeping. "We'd gotten back from Paris, and my daughter and her husband were staying in a little cottage that sits on my property. Matthew had told me that he had to do two weeks of training in Manhattan—he had started taking some film courses as a hobby—and he was going to be staying with his buddy. I'd come downstairs late that morning, and around nine o'clock or so, my son-in-law walked into the house. He said, in this funny tone of voice, 'You know, Mom, I was up early, and Matthew was bringing stuff into the car, so I helped him. He took an awful lot of stuff, way too much for someone who was just going for two weeks.' And so all of a sudden I thought 'Huh!' I literally walked around the kitchen going 'Huh!' It was clear to me what had just happened . . . he'd left." Her voice had dropped to that hushed, scared tone I'd heard on the telephone.

"So it wasn't a mutual decision. He just took off without telling you," I said.

"No, he did not tell me. Needless to say, I was shocked out of my mind. And strangely enough, to this day, the thing that I struggle with is—despite the fact that I understand in many ways why we are not together—I still can't believe it." Tears stood in her eyes momentarily; then she sucked them back.

Now an entire piece of her life had vanished. Gabe, the stepson she had spent so much time taking care of, was grown and gone. He was a lawyer working in New York City, but she never heard from him. "I think that he had everything to do with the demise of our marriage. It's not his fault, but I think if there were any chance of Matthew and me getting together again, it wouldn't happen because of him."

"Why is that?" I asked, and Julie's face tightened. "Because Matthew puts him on a pedestal. He thinks his son is a god and that he comes first and foremost before anyone else. Throughout our marriage, that was the case. I suppose Gabe must have had some tender feelings for me. He cried when we told him, during a restaurant dinner, that we were divorcing—but from that point on, he simply disappeared. He's never called me to ask how I was doing. Also, he'd been close to his stepsister, Leslie, at one time, but he's called my daughter maybe once in the past year."

"It must be very hurtful," I said quietly. My thought was that even with Matthew's son gone from the household, his powerful, divisive influence had remained.

"It's so painful, I can't tell you. What's painful is that a whole period of my life, which ended up being close to twenty years, it has all vanished—poof!" Julie pursed her lips as if blowing a bubble into the air. "Gabe's not in my life; Fran, Matthew's ex, is not in my life; Matthew is barely in my life. We still talk on the telephone now and then, though he's living in Amsterdam, at least for the meanwhile. Nobody speaks to my daughter, though she was considered part of that family for eighteen years while I was with my ex-husband."

I learned that Matthew's former wife, Fran, was now remarried, and the two women's friendship had long since dissipated. "She never even called when she heard we had split up." Julie sounded desolate. Her parents were dead now, and so was her only sister, she told me.

She was silent for a moment, then said, "I still can't take it in, can't accept it as real . . . every single one of them, gone." She looked like an abandoned castaway, someone standing alone in a space that was filled with rubble.

Without Authority

During my earlier interviews with the Albrights, both members of the couple were consciously aware of their difficulties and were squaring off about their relational conflicts openly. Julie was making futile efforts to help her husband understand how awful it felt to be eternally second best— the "mother" of a stepson whom she was never permitted to mother, since his "real" mother lived nearby and remained the person in complete authority.

Matthew, still much affected by the myth of instant love, was bitterly defensive when it came to Gabe. He considered it a personal failing of Julie's that she hadn't immediately joined him in creating the ideal family that he'd dreamed of during the romantic time of their courtship. He felt as if she'd tricked him by not feeling the way he'd fully expected her to feel.

The couple's difficulties were compounded when they consulted a famed family therapist who was unschooled in the dynamics of stepfamily life. The therapist counseled Julie to leave all the mothering to Gabe's "real" mother, while Julie herself apparently

was accorded no role in the family whatsoever. This was not helpful advice for a remarried family suffering from this kind of distress and confusion.

"That brilliant family systems therapist neutered me," Julie
said now. "I was never allowed to have any authority with his son
while Matthew was there. When Matthew wasn't around, the two
of us managed reasonably well. But if a dispute ever developed
when Matthew was there . . ." She let her thought dangle.

I smiled. "You were in the wrong."

"Exactly! And Matthew would never step in. He would say,
'That's between the two of you. I have nothing to do with it.
Work it out.' So after what that therapist had advised, the whole
thing was doomed." I paused, reflecting upon how hard it must
have been to be stuck on the outside of that intimately connected
blood-related system for almost two decades of her lifetime.

I was bemused by the fact Gabe had continued to have such
power over the marriage, considering that he was now grown and
gone from the household. When I asked Julie about this, she
shrugged and said that perhaps it was because her own relationship with him was infantile; it had never really developed. This
made me wonder if Julie, "neutered" out of an active role in the
parenting of her stepson, had been jealous of him as a pseudo-sib-
ling, someone who was vying for and commandeering her husband's attention.

At that moment, she heaved a deep sigh, as if a poignant memory had stirred her. "Matthew was back from Amsterdam in February. He stayed in the cottage next to the house, and we had
three nice, friendly days. It was snowing, and we were really cozy.
There was no physical contact, although I have to say"—she hesitated—"it's still there when he walks into a room—that same
chemistry that I had before. I think he has it too, but it's way too
dangerous to think about doing anything like that."

She shrugged as if to dismiss the very idea. "The fact remains
there is still a softness and a tenderness. We'd been through a

divorce, and yet he stayed next door, and we had those three nice days . . ." Her voice trailed off, then she added glumly that on the last day, they'd had a huge fight. "We were sitting in a restaurant in Darien, and Matthew said he thought he was going to get a tattoo. I said, 'Oh, cool. What are you going to put on yourself?' And he said that he was going to put 'Gabriel' on his arm. I was just flabbergasted, because to me that symbolized all of the pain I'd been through.

"I said to him, 'Of all of the things in the world that you've learned, and all that you've been through in your sixty-five years, that name is the one you're going to carve into your flesh?' That just said it all. There's no room for me!" Her voice had risen to a high note of outrage—the voice of the furious, impotent outsider.

It was very strange: even after the divorce, she was still vying for the position of number one in her ex-husband's world. Clearly, the Albrights had never made it past their early conflicts about Gabe. They had simply remained in a state of overt or covert combat for eighteen difficult years together. And in Paris, the original biological system had finally thrust her from the scene completely.

A Downward Financial Spiral

Julie's personal finances had taken a serious reversal in the great recession of 2008. "I lost a lot of money. I lost more than half of what I had," she told me dejectedly. She was still able, supplemented by her school psychologist's salary, to maintain her home and live in a relatively spartan kind of comfort. Her own portfolio—separate from her ex-husband's after the divorce—had been more diversified than his had been, so she had found herself in a relatively better position after that precipitous drop in the stock market.

"By that time Matthew had left the business in which he'd partnered with his ex-wife, and he'd moved to a well-known wealth management firm. They loved him there, and he moved up the ranks at top speed. He became a principal in record time and was considered one of their stars. So, in late February he called me and said, 'We are going to make so much money this year, it's unbelievable.' Then a week later, he called again and told me that he'd been fired. I said, 'What?' And he said that they'd fired him and escorted him out of the building."

Julie was in the dark about what had happened. I asked her what Matthew's financial situation was then and at this moment. She said that it had been all right at that time, for he'd received a decent settlement. "But you probably remember the way he was—a high-roller, a huge risk taker. When the recession hit, he'd leveraged most of his assets in stocks, one hundred percent. He was wiped out."

Matthew was now sharing an apartment in Amsterdam with a couple of Dutch friends, but before leaving, he had stayed on in his Park Avenue condo, with its $3,500 monthly rent, while collecting unemployment insurance. When I asked Julie how he was supporting himself now, she shrugged and raised her arms into the air.

"Unemployment insurance, I suppose. He has no money. I don't know what happens to him in the dead of night when he has a lucid moment, but he seems to be not at all worried. I speak with him on the telephone fairly often, and he talks as if he can get a job whenever he wants one. But who is going to hire him? When he was sixty-five and got fired he could still have gotten a great job because he is a brilliant salesman with an incredible résumé. But the recession came along, and nobody is hiring people like that now. The strange thing is that it doesn't seem to bother him."

It was Julie who sounded worried and Julie who sounded as if she cared. The relationship had been painful, and she had always felt shut out. Still, it was clear that she hadn't yet left the marriage behind her.

Houses

When I met with Matthew Albright several weeks later, he was not wearing the kind of bohemian outfit, complete with gold chains, that Julie had led me to anticipate. Instead, he arrived in a plain white button-down shirt and neat trousers. It was early June. At age sixty-five (thirteen years after I'd last seen him), Matthew was still a fine-looking man—so tall that he seemed to dominate the low-ceilinged room. He had put on a bit of weight, mostly around the belly, and his light brown hair was receding slightly around the temples. Still, he was an attractive, surprisingly relaxed presence.

I realized that I'd expected to find him much more changed than he was, given the reversals that he'd experienced. At the time of our first interviews, he was a wealthy man, living in a beautiful, light-drenched house on the Connecticut shoreline. He was now (as far as his ex-wife knew) a virtual pauper, trying to forge a new life in a foreign country. It seemed to me to be a young man's game, not something to commence in one's sixties.

I began our interview by asking Matthew the same opening question I had asked Julie: "What happened?" After so many years together, what had broken their long remarriage apart?

He stared at me for a moment and then said, "I reached a point where I thought my life was so joyless. I thought my life was going to end."

I was taken aback. "How many years had you been married when you began getting these feelings? It was certainly a very vibrant relationship when I first interviewed you." I thought of their assurances at that time that this marriage was forever. I waited before saying, "Appearances can be deceptive."

He didn't take me up on this last remark. "No, I think it was very vibrant and exciting. It was always volatile. Always. But I think the trouble took root when I realized Julie's feelings about the house on the shore. It didn't suit her. It made her really unhappy, and it was very special to me—probably the most creative thing I ever did in my life. I'd met her just about the time it was completed, and over time, she coerced me into moving out of that house. In retrospect, I was really traumatized by that."

"What was her objection to the house?"

Matthew's left foot had begun jiggling up and down, a sign of edginess I recalled from years earlier. "It wasn't 'cozy' enough." He gave the word "cozy" a sarcastic spin. He then added that the house on the shore was heavily mortgaged, and the consulting business he'd co-owned with his ex-wife, Fran, and a third partner wasn't doing too well at that time; it always had its ups and downs. The most important factor was, however, Julie's unhappiness. "She wanted 'cozy' and I wanted to please her. So I put the house up for sale."

One day the agent who was handling the sale of the shoreline house had called Matthew and told him of an old Victorian home that was going on the market the next day. "I ran by the house, and said, 'This is the place for Julie.' So I bought it, and called her and said I'd just signed the contract. She came by, and she fell in love with the place. It was perfect for her—very handsome, mature plantings. It was on a hill, but as it turned out, there were a million things wrong with it. It made no sense: small, small rooms. And dark. Not open and bright and light—just the opposite. In my desire to gratify Julie's needs, I ran roughshod over my own."

To top off his discomfiture, he had fallen down the stairs on the first night of their occupancy. The risers on the stairs were much narrower than the ones in the house on the shore that he had built. Now Matthew's jiggling foot was tapping a louder, more insistent rhythm.

He said that Julie had felt lost from day one in the shoreline home that felt so right to him. "She just kept on me about how we have to sell this house, we have to sell this house," he said, his voice tinged with anger.

I asked him how long before the marriage ended they had bought the cozy house.

He thought for a moment, said it must have been about six or seven years—about the time that he had left the partnership with Fran. "I left because Julie was clearly displeased by the fact that it wasn't going well," he said. In Matthew's mind, Julie was to blame for many of the unwise steps that he had taken.

"I thought your first wife was a best friend of hers," I said.

Matthew laughed a brief, sarcastic laugh. "Never best friends."

"We talked about that in our earlier interviews." I raised an eyebrow.

Matthew shrugged. "I believe you if you say so. But I'm going to say that in reality, they were never really friends." His tone of voice implied that whatever Julie might have believed, the two women had never shared any kind of true friendship whatsoever.

Critical Junctures

Although selling the house on the shoreline had marked a critical downturn in the Albrights' relationship, something that had occurred much earlier had far outweighed it in importance. Said Matthew, "A moment in time that I point to is that not long after we were married, I was able to convince Fran that joint custody of Gabe would be best for everybody involved."

"Julie had a grown daughter then. Was she interested in taking care of another child?" I asked, then added, "Was she in on that decision?"

Matthew's face flushed slightly. "No, she wasn't—not in a major way—and that was a huge bone of contention."

I said I thought that it would be, given the fact that he was traveling a great deal. "After all, she was going to be the person in charge when you weren't on the scene."

Matthew paused, then said he now realized that Julie's being unaware of an impending custody change might not have been a good idea. "When we first married, the arrangement was that I would see Gabe every Wednesday and every other weekend, but basically he would be living with his mother. But Fran and I talked things out after the marriage, and we came to a joint decision—to share custody of our son. Could Julie have influenced that decision in any way? I would say no, to this day. That was my decision. I would not have allowed anyone to influence the decision that I made." His voice had taken on a defiant tone.

"Not even your new wife?" I asked.

"Nobody," he said definitively.

"In other words, your parenting was more important than being a spouse? That's what I'm hearing you say."

"Yes, I would feel the same way to this day! I might do things somewhat differently, in retrospect, but I would always feel that way."

I nodded and said that had surely been a tricky development—giving someone care of his child without allowing her any input or advance warning. "You would certainly see that now," I said, and he nodded his head in agreement.

"So that arrangement, like the house, was another point of contention. You said that there was a series of junctures where you came up against issues that you thought became unresolvable?"

Matthew was quiet for a moment and then wrung his hands together. He said that going over this material was like having a root canal, because at some level he still loved Julie and thought he always would. Then he cleared his throat. Another major issue, he said—one that had emerged shortly after the remarriage—was his new wife's unhappiness with how much he was traveling.

I asked him how much he had been traveling. "Probably a lot," he acknowledged, sometimes two or even three weeks out of every month. "It could have been leaving on a Sunday and getting back on a Thursday," he admitted.

I smiled, said that his having joint custody meant Julie's having joint custody, in the sense that he was absent so often. "Did you realize that was going to happen?" I asked him.

He hesitated, looked uncomfortable, said that he and Fran had tried to structure their travels so that one parent would be there when the other was absent. "But it wasn't unusual that we would both be away at the same time. On business."

So then Julie would be in charge?"

He shrugged his shoulders, didn't answer.

"So when Julie was in charge, was she empowered in the same way a babysitter would be empowered—for instance, 'Here are the rules and regulations,' and while the parent is away she is the person to enforce them? Was that the deal for her?"

He hesitated. "Great question. I don't want to sound defensive, because that was a real mess, handled badly. And to cut to the core of the problem, Julie wanted a parenting role, not a babysitting role."

I wasn't clear about the distinction he was making. In my own experience, a babysitter is someone who takes charge of the children and is entrusted with the parent's authority during times when the parents are away. I said so to Matthew, adding with a softening smile, "The children can't be in charge of the babysitter. Is there some confusion about this?"

"No," he said shortly.

After a long pause, I asked him if Julie had been volatile with his son.

"I would have to guess," he answered slowly, "but no, I don't think you could ever use that term in regard to her. They didn't get along in the sense that he did not like her. It didn't really matter at that age. Gabe was doing very well in school, he was a good student."

"But he was spending a lot of time with someone he didn't like," I pointed out. Matthew nodded his agreement and said he hadn't realized this until much later.

My thought was that the old biological system hadn't budged a bit when Julie Albright entered the family's life, and consequently, she had never become the mistress of her own household. Whatever her illusions (Matthew's unfailing devotion and her best-friendship with Fran) had been during our earlier interviews, I was now learning that she'd always been the distrusted, disliked stranger in the family—far more than she knew.

Despite their long years together and the fact that her ex-husband still had deep feelings for her, Matthew had never been able to empathize with how lonely and disrespected her outsider's position had really made her feel.

Gabe

It was hard to overlook the real losses that seven-year-old Gabe Albright had suffered by the time that Julie came into his life. The children of divorce are deeply shaken by the breakup of the original family, and the fantasy that their own parents will reunite is ever present. Such fantasies often persist long after any realistic possibility has vanished from sight. Undoubtedly, Matthew's remarriage must have been experienced as a blow to the boy's deepest, most fervent desires.

Following that crucial event, the joint custody agreement resulted in Gabe's being bounced out of his mother's home far more frequently and left in the care of a stepmother who was probably as displeased by the changed situation as he must have been. This new arrangement was still a further falling off for the young boy who was also being informed, sotto voce, that Julie wasn't his "real" mother and he didn't have to listen to her. Gabe was simply being warehoused with her on the frequent occasions when both his parents were away on business trips.

Now, these many years and a failed remarriage later, the entire matter was moot. I was struck, however, by how much Julie and Matthew still seemed to care for each other. Their marriage was over without actually being over. At one point during our interview, Matthew heaved a deep sigh, then actually said, "It's funny, I walk into that house and I fall in love with her all over again. Just like that. I mean I adore her."

I thought about Julie's remark to the effect that Gabe was to some large degree the cause of the demise of their marriage and the major reason she and her ex-spouse would never reunite. So I asked Matthew, my voice tone tentative, "Would any of the issues relating to Gabe prevent you and Julie from ever getting back together again? Would he be a source of contention between you?"

The question seemed to take him by surprise. "Gabe is twenty-eight years old," he stated, as if my question was completely ridiculous.

"A twenty-eight-year-old can still be an issue," I answered mildly. "But you don't think that would be the case?"

This time Matthew stopped and thought the matter over. "If I called him up and said I was getting back with Julie, his first reaction would be to say, 'You can't be serious, right?' And I would say, 'No, I'm very serious,' and he would say, 'All right, I suppose you know what you're doing.'" There was another long pause, and then Matthew said, "When I think about it, Gabe is certainly in the forefront of my mind when I imagine how he'd react and what he would say."

"I'm hearing that you think he would disapprove and think you were acting like a jerk," I said. The remark itself was a question—one that was met with a long silence, a silence that was an implicit answer.

THINKING ABOUT THE ALBRIGHTS

What fundamental errors and misjudgments had led to the sad ending of this, in some curious way, still loving couple's marriage? Clearly, the parenting tasks challenge had figured prominently in corroding the substructure of the relationship. The very thought of returning to Julie made Matthew think of how embarrassed he would be in front of his son, and Julie herself believed Gabe was the major obstacle to their ever reconnecting again.

To some significant degree it seemed to me that a grave, almost insuperable problem had been created by the therapist the Albrights had consulted early in the game. This clinician, then a leading figure in family therapy, had obviously been working with a first-family model in her mind. She didn't appear to have had a clue about how to deal with the complex issues and challenges that remarried families must confront and master. Her advice—that Julie was to have no voice whatsoever in regard to Gabe's caretaking—had reduced this second wife to a role that might be best described as "Matthew's married mistress."

If, throughout the years of her marriage, Julie continued to feel "like an amorphous kind being," an add-on, it was because she was never truly admitted into the family circle. Despite their divorce, Matthew and first wife Fran were the only parents/adults in the picture and the only real authorities recognized by their son. Therefore the core challenge of remarriage—bringing the outsider(s) into an insider position in a newly restructured family system—was one at which the remarried Albrights had failed.

Gabe was never really asked to shift his loyalties from Fran to Julie, so he probably felt little conflict on that score. But on the other hand, his hurts and losses were never fully addressed. His devoted dad had told me in our final interview that Gabe had never really liked Julie. Had it taken the boy's loving parents a lifetime to find out how their child really felt? And if they'd known this, why had they continued to leave Gabe in Julie's care for such extended periods of time?

When it came to the challenge of the other parent, it was clearly true that Matthew's first wife had never left the domestic scene. Although Fran's love for her ex-husband was obviously not reciprocated—and he had already been remarried for eight years at the time of our interviews—loving Matthew appeared to have remained the key focus of her emotional existence. It was Fran's still-powerful feelings for him that served to make sense not only of her personal history but of her daily life in the present. So, as Julie's "new best friend" and as Gabe's other ("real") parent, she had taken up her residence at the very center of this feckless step-couple's existence.

CHAPTER TWO

Constructing
the Architectural Model

What can a couple's remarrying have to do with the subject of architecture? According to Patricia Papernow, the model's creator and one of America's foremost experts on stepfamily dynamics, the answer to this question is by now a familiar one: later marriages differ from first-time-ever marriages in terms of their fundamental structure their basic blueprint for living. Although not every remarriage will conform to the architectural model, the huge majority of second or later marriages do. Moreover, when it comes to remarriages that are running into trouble, an understanding of this remarkable model is essential.

First of all, there is no more lucid theoretical framework for understanding the particular challenges confronting remarrying pairs. Second, and equally important, this model comes fortified by a variety of research-based strategies (some are counterintuitive) that can prove invaluable as the re-wed partners struggle to create a comfortable, inclusive place for all members of the new family that their remarriage has created.

THE HISTORY OF A MARRIAGE

How are remarried couples, deeply troubled by one or more of the five major challenges posited by the architectural model, to deal realistically with these hurdles? In order to respond to this question we'll look at the ways in which the intact first-time family begins and how it develops over time.

I shall use as an example a typical couple named Jenny and Bill Blakeslee. When Jenny and Bill married, they were in their late twenties. Their marriage entailed, as marriages do, a huge transition involving a shift in all the relationships that formerly comprised their single-adult reality. Now the newly committed pair must set about creating a private sphere that becomes the special province of the two people involved.

To be sure, each member of the couple has come into the marriage with a different autobiography. The differing family cultures from which they sprang have impressed certain ideas and beliefs into their psyches. Although the partners may share certain values, beliefs, and religious practices, their ideas and preferences are unlikely to fit together in a lock-and-key fashion. For example, Jenny might love the beach and the ocean (where her family always vacationed), while Bill prefers hiking in the mountains (which he did every summer at camp). Each partner has to adapt to the other partner's cherished views, preferences, and notions. If things have been going well, and one of the mates is not trying to trump the other's reality by insisting that they should *both* want things his or her own way, their new vacation will probably consist of a compromise—for instance, a ramble through the Blue Ridge Mountains of Virginia that ends at the seashore in North Carolina.

As the Blakeslees' marital conversation goes on, from bed to breakfast table to work to leisure activities, they will be—consciously and unconsciously—working out a mutually agreeable set of behaviors; that is, establishing common ground. This is the couple's own culture, their established ways of doing things. It consists of dozens of implicit, mutually agreed-upon understandings ranging from, "Do you begin eating dinner before the other has started?" to "What do you do with the towels after taking your shower?" to "How much emotional closeness and how much distance feel comfortable?"

Throughout this period, the couple has been in the process of establishing their own unique territory—the way things are and the way things are done in the private culture that is their own relationship. And over time, as they work through their inevitable differences, the Blakeslees' shared common ground expands like a slowly accumulating sand dune.

Clearly, a great difference between this first-time pair and a remarrying couple is that the first-marriage Blakeslees will have a period alone in which to create the roles, rules, and rituals—and iron out the differences—that make up the warp and woof of their own private world. Their experience of early wedlock is very different from that of a stepparent who is often startled to find herself plumped down in the middle of a family culture that she doesn't really understand—one in which incomprehensible animosities can be triggered by the most innocuous-seeming request or remark.

Time Alone

A first-time couple like the Blakeslees luxuriates in that precious private time in which to reach out; to make love whenever the spirit strikes them; to have long, drifting conversations; to get more and more connected; and at the same time, to develop some behavioral habits together. Bill has studied classical piano, and Jenny isn't particularly musical, but they both enjoy folk music and ballads. So when they're driving somewhere, they sing their favorite songs together, including some German lieder Bill has taught his bride (even though Jenny can barely carry a tune). On some weekends, the new partners practice the rudiments of camping out, and Jenny learns to enjoy mountain hikes in ways she never has before. They both love to laze around and read the entire *New York Times* on Sunday afternoons.

In the first year or two together, the mates will have sufficient leisure in which to teach each other more of their favorite folk songs and have fun broadening their shared American and foreign repertoire. Over time they will figure out how best to set up a campsite together, and Jenny, who is an excellent swimmer, will give Bill some pointers on his stroke. Together, the members of the couple create an area of comfort—common ground—in which both can operate easily and almost automatically with little thought or effort.

The Blakeslees' patterns for living are in place, and when their first child is born, she enters into an emotional and behavioral family world that is already well established. Now old songs they learned as children may be sung as lullabies, and the baby may be taken on walks or hikes in her daddy's backpack. A host of parenting differences between the partners may become evident as their infant ages—for instance, discordant views about what a reasonable bedtime is and whether discipline consists of a time-out or a whack on the child's rear end. One partner may emerge as the disciplinary "heavy," while the other is the overly permissive "good guy." However, since both members of the couple love their offspring, their common ground thickens, and they survive the jolting changes that accompany parenthood.

In a first-time family like the Blakeslees, the children will be added one by one, and the family will have sufficient time to struggle with each new set of relationships. There is enough middle or common ground in place to help them figure out how to deal with new problems by learning from their successes and mistakes.

In a subsequent marriage, however, there will be no such latitude of alone time for the pair. The remarried couple will never enjoy a leisurely period by themselves in which to establish a strong connection and will share a scanty common ground of shared associations and taken-for-granted understandings. They will never have the chance to become acquainted with each child in the family seriatim, from earliest infancy onward.

On the contrary, the stranger/stepparent enters the family—which has been sundered by divorce or by death—as if she or he has slid down the chimney and landed in the center of an ongoing emotional and behavioral world where the oldest, strongest connections are those shared by the children and the biological parent.

The End of a Familiar Civilization

When a family experiences a marital breakup, many of their long-established rhythms of being and behaving—their common ground—are lost. For the children, this brings about the incredible ending of the family world as they have always known it. The rupture may also involve the children's moving to a new school, a reduction in the custodial parent's (typically the mother's) income, and a lessening degree of empathic connection on the part of one or both parents, for they themselves are often preoccupied by their own feelings of dislocation. The adults are experiencing the loss of the marriage and the family just as intensely as their offspring and are struggling to establish a new emotional equilibrium. One or both adults may be feeling as emotionally needy as their children do.

As author Pat Conroy observes, "Every divorce marks the death of a small civilization." For the youngsters, this transition from first-time family to broken family is a shocking, unthinkable experience. It is freighted with many fears, especially that of being uncared for in a confusingly large, fragmented adult universe.

However, it is known that if divorcing partners can shield their offspring from too much venomous and open conflict, the children may surmount the hardships of this alarmingly unstable time of their lives. *Parental conflict is the key.* The amount and intensity of adult strife to which the children are exposed will make the difference between whether they can continue to develop normally or will begin to fail in school or act out in other self-destructive ways.

Unfortunately it is true that many ex-mates find it difficult, if not impossible, to refrain from bad-mouthing the former spouse or the new stepparent and dragging their children into the marital fray. These angry ex-mates are obviously unaware of the substantial research literature underlining the fact that parental fighting (whether the pair is married, separated, or divorced) has damaging effects upon their children's emotional growth and later adjustment.

In the wake of the first-time marriage's demise, much of the original family's familiar common ground will have become dispersed, though some aspects of "the way things used to be" will remain. In the case of the Blakeslees, who did eventually divorce, Jenny has continued to sing familiar folk songs when she is driving, although her two daughters giggle about her inability to carry a tune. Bill is always obliging about bringing his girls to the seashore, although everyone knows he wants to leave early because he can't bear sitting in the sun doing nothing for very long.

"In any event, we now have two single-parent families," remarriage expert Papernow told me during our many conversations, "and over time, single-parent families work out their own ways of operating, their own rhythms of being." For instance, Bill and his two daughters, now eight and ten, may have developed something they call "Italian Night." One of their grandmothers is Italian and has taught the girls how to make wonderful meatballs. So the children come over on most Wednesday evenings, drop their backpacks, and start fashioning the meatballs while Dad works on cooking the red sauce. They then prepare a potful of linguine, set the table with grated cheese and hot-pepper flakes, and dig into their favorite dinner together. Later on, Dad washes the dishes, and his daughters dry them while chattering away about their friends and schoolwork.

When the kitchen work is finished, one or both of the children may ask for help with homework problems. On some evenings, if they have managed to complete their lessons quickly, the girls will watch a program on TV or a short, juvenile-oriented movie before their bedtime. Since both Bill and his daughters enjoy Italian Night enormously, it soon becomes a reliable part of their new common ground, "our family's accustomed way of spending Wednesday evenings at Dad's house." Rituals of this kind bring a measure of stability to the children's lives.

"Then"—Dr. Papernow rolled her wide brown eyes as if to say trouble was coming—"Bill begins dating and gets increasingly serious about someone new."

The first-time family's common ground, its ways of being that have accrued over time, sustained serious disruptions when Bill and Jenny parted ways. The common ground that grew up between this single-parent father and his two young daughters was established in the wake of this event. When the stepparent, Anne, enters the picture, she is the outsider to all of this. She and Bill may share a powerful, exciting new attachment, but there is an older, deeper connection between the man she married and his children that has preceded her on the scene. Although the stepparent may be filled with good intentions for blending easily into her new husband's family and being a good mother to his daughters, she is unaware that she has entered a foreign culture whose folkways she doesn't begin to comprehend.

MAGGIE SCARF

MEETING THE CHALLENGES

The architectural model serves as a quick way for troubled remarried partners to understand and find a language for the nature of their present dilemmas and their goals for the future. Thinking about the five different challenges and the different ways in which the partners can meet those challenges provides a crisp set of working diagrams for making structural changes.

The changes desired are completely unlike any first-marriage family design, although many newly remarried partners start out with that first-time model in their minds—which is why "instant blending" is such a widespread yet unrealistic expectation. Actually, the remarriage experience is comparable to trying to find your way through a dimly lit, unfamiliar building, wrenching open an unmarked door and finding yourself tumbling down a cellar stairway. In other words, trying to use a first-marriage blueprint as you attempt to find your way into a later marriage is frequently a confusing, disorienting experience.

Challenge One: Insider/Outsider Positions

The first (and perhaps the core) challenge, into which all others feed, is what Papernow terms the remarried couple's "stuck insider" and "stuck outsider" positions. These positions are built into the basic structure of later marriages, for children are born hardwired to form a powerful attachment to their biological parents. The stepparent enters the household as a stranger to this profound connection and she or he is hampered by ignorance of the daily rhythms (common ground) that the mate's single-parent household has developed in the interval following the breakup.

It is clearly true that the common ground between parent and child is far better established than the relatively fragile common ground forged in a new couple's relationship. The remarried part-ners may be mutually entranced, but there is a powerful, dense attachment that exists between parent and child. There is no such thick, historically based bond between the stepparent and the new mate and surely no such bond shared by the stepparent and his or her spouse's children. Therefore, he or she occupies the unenviable role of the stuck outsider to the family when the new marriage begins.

In this marital schema, there is no time for the couple to get to know one another slowly, in their own exclusive world, for the children and the family culture are already in place and demand the biological parent's attention. Thus, early in the remarriage, the newcomer is likely to start feeling isolated and like a family add-on; someone who is fixed in her outsider position and is not being invited inside as a member of the solidly established group to which her partner belongs.

According to Papernow, this first period of stepfamily life may see huge disagreements blow up over seemingly trivial issues, which in her view are usually poorly disguised stuck insider/stuck outsider issues. Perhaps the stepparent loves Grape Nuts, which she considers a healthy food, but her stepchildren consider it a form of cardboard. Papernow herself is remarried to a man with three children of his own, and she is the mother of one daugh-ter. She smiled and told me that when she put Grape Nuts on the table, she was informed testily that her husband's family ate only sugary cereals for breakfast (which she considered a form of dessert).

This difference became a source of ongoing disagreement as the stuck outsider (Patricia) tried to have a voice in deciding the breakfast menu, while the stuck insider (her new husband) strug-gled to keep her feeling included while reassuring his children that they would not have to deal with more changes and adjust-ments in their lives—they had been through so many already.

In a remarried family, the easy paths to agreement about what is a good breakfast cereal and a host of other daily decisions (the behavioral common ground) are shared by the stuck-insider parent and his children. This renders the stepparent the stuck outsider, for she feels invisible, without a voice in the ongoing life of the family. What to do?

Couples dealing with these issues, asserts Papernow, need to have them highlighted and normalized by means of psychoeducation. In her view, many remarriages fall into states of distress because the partners are simply uninformed about the nature of later marriages and hurry to the altar anticipating instant blended felicity from the moment of the wedding onward. The remarrying couple may be very much in love but they are far from clear-eyed, and when they enter the new relationship they often have airy, unrealistic expectations.

So sooner or later—but probably sooner—when they meet with disappointments and feelings of exclusion or, alternatively, "being torn to pieces" by competing claims on their time and affections, they start to blame the partner and to doubt the relationship itself. In many instances, says the expert, they are confronting the basic architecture of remarriage rather than a truly irreparable marital choice.

They need to be taught about the underlying structure of remarriage (most pronounced in the early years), which has inevitably shifted them into stuck-insider and stuck-outsider positions. They must also develop some sincere empathy for the other partner's position. The stuck-insider partner needs to comprehend what it's like to have one's wishes and needs routinely ignored when certain changes in the way the family system operates are requested. The stuck-outsider partner must use her imagination to understand how overwhelming it can feel to keep negotiating the flare-ups between his or her cherished, dependent children and the beloved new partner he or she has introduced into the household.

The stuck outsider may well believe that the insider partner's life is all roses, because everyone in the family is vying for his or her caring and attention. But actually the insider position is highly distressing because he or she is feeling beset by conflicting demands— unable to please the treasured new spouse, who wants to have a voice and make some changes in the family, and unable to please the children, who have suffered so many psychic blows and hard transitions and are resistant to making any changes whatsoever.

COMPARTMENTALIZE, COMPARTMENTALIZE, COMPARTMENTALIZE

If highly polarized stuck insider/stuck outsider positions are built into the architecture of remarriage, what are smart ways of dealing with the problems they tend to create? First, as mentioned above, learning that this is so helps to normalize the difficulties the new couple is likely to be having. Second, partners in distress are greatly relieved by simply finding the words with which to describe the confusing, painful feelings they are experiencing.

As Papernow writes, "Outsiders feel constantly left out, rejected, and lonely . . . [while] . . . insiders feel torn, inadequate, even desperate." The phrase *blended family* does not prepare for reality the couple who shared the happy fantasy that they and their offspring would engage in lots of fun activities and swiftly merge into a much happier family than the previous one(s) had been. Normalizing insider/outsider dilemmas and letting go of illusions of instant blending propel the new couple a giant step forward from the miserable place in which they were blaming one another and doubting the viability of the new relationship.

A somewhat different strategy for dealing with the challenges posed by remarriage architecture is one that seems quite paradoxical and counterintuitive. Says Papernow: "Many people believe they can resolve their 'blending' issues by spending a lot of time with the entire family present. However, the truth is that when you are all together as a family these issues are at their most intense: Insider/outsider issues are at their most intense; kids feel most displaced and subject to loyalty binds; and the parenting challenges and cultural differences are at their most intense too."

The most helpful way of dealing with these structural problems is, in Papernow's words, to "compartmentalize, compartmentalize, compartmentalize." That is, carve out space and time for one-to-one relationships across the family spectrum.

The biological parent-child duo should have time alone, because the kids do need that ongoing, consistent connection with the parent. The stepparent/child pair should also have time alone, because while this new family member is viewed as a big plus by the spouse, he or she is often experienced as a minus by the children: he or she is an outlander, whom they didn't have a voice in choosing. Moreover, this new arrival undoubtedly involves some lessening of the parent's attentiveness (he or she is in love) and some changes in the rhythm of daily life. Such changes are hard to deal with for these youngsters, who have dealt with many losses and upheavals already. The new family member's appearance on the domestic scene is also highly likely to stir up some feelings of competition and resentment.

The stepparent and the spouse's children need to get to know one another much better, so perhaps she or he and a stepdaughter might go to a movie or go shopping together. Perhaps the stepparent can take the partner's son to a sporting event (without the boy's parent coming along) or ask the youngster to teach him or her a skill. For instance, the stepson might show the family newcomer how to Tweet or establish a presence on Facebook. The stepparent could spend some time playing a board game or helping a younger child with homework. In short, the lately arrived "parent" and the child or children need to get connected with one another on a one-to-one basis, which they can do best when the biological parent isn't present or at least is not overseeing the activity.

Last, but certainly far from least, the remarried spouses should carve out "insider" time to spend together—time that will be uninterrupted by the youngsters' issues, difficulties, and demands. They might take a regular evening out, especially before non-custodial children are to appear on the scene. "You do have to put energy into the stepcouple," says Papernow. "But what the research shows very clearly is that what works best is arranging for one-to-one time throughout the entire family. *Compartmentalize*," she reiterates, "and use that one-to-one time to establish good connections."

Challenge Two: Children's Losses and Loyalty Binds

Most manuals of advice for remarried partners stress the importance of the couple's interpersonal relationship. There is a widespread, much-touted belief that if the mates are managing their own marriage well, the rest of the family members will soon fall into place, and a happy, well blended group will soon emerge. The architectural model is different in that it takes seriously the fact that the biological parent's gain—his or her new romantic partner—is often experienced by his or her children as yet another in a series of family calamities and stressful transitions.

For this reason, Papernow suggests that the stepparent initiate very few new rules of order and changes at the outset of the marriage—and that such changes be directed mainly at maintaining civility. For example, a stepchild should be required to look at the stepparent and say "Hello" when entering a room rather than greeting the biological parent and pretending that this new person (the spouse) is not even present.

Another challenge regarding the children of remarriage has to do with conflicts of loyalty. A child may brood endlessly over such issues as, "If I like [or get to love] my stepparent, am I betraying my real [biological] parent?" Or if the biological parent has died, the child may ponder the question, "If I start to love my stepparent, will my memories of my real parent start to fade?" A wonderful way of dealing with this sort of issue directly can be found in a little document of Papernow's that she calls "Patricia's script." This statement (or some variation of it) could be useful for a divorced and remarried parent like Bill Blakeslee to introduce when he is chatting with his resentful, troubled eleven-year-old daughter during a quiet bedtime conversation:

> Having a stepmom and a mom can be confusing to a lot of kids. I want you to know that your mom's place in your heart is permanent. Like the earth. Like the sun. Just like your place in your mom's heart is permanent. Your mom will always be your mom. You will always be her daughter. Anne is different from your mom. A stepmom is different from a mom. I hope you will come to care for Anne as time goes on, but if you do, your relationship with her will always be in a different place in your heart from your relationship with your mom.

The comforting notion that the biological parent and the stepparent can occupy different places in a heart that is large enough to house them both is a way of assuaging and putting to rest the child's guilt and uneasy sense of duplicity.

Challenge Three: Parenting Tasks

As noted above, single-parent families tend to become more permissive families, and over time, the boundary between the child and the adult generation begins to seem indistinct. Often one or more of the youngsters moves very close to the parent, almost unconsciously, in order to fill the empty space the other parent once occupied. In a variety of ways, the children gain a degree of power that they would never have had if the first-time family had remained intact.

This accrued power comes in tandem with being needed, becoming more of a confidant, taking on extra responsibilities (perhaps the care of younger siblings), and helping out more around the household. In the course of ordinary events the children move up a notch while the parent moves downward in terms of his or her familial power and authority.

When the stepparent enters the domestic scene, he or she may be taken aback by the laxness and malleability of the household rules. She or he has now found her- or himself in an overly close, biologically bonded family, one that seems to lack respect for the adults' authority. As a result, the stepparent tends to move into a more authoritarian, hard-line position. These are not *her* children, and they're often not particularly friendly to her. They may be letting her know that they're not too thrilled to have her there by ignoring her requests or by defying her openly.

Eventually the stepparent becomes distressed by the children's dismissive behavior or outright rudeness, and she wants her mate to exert his authority—to step up to the plate and do something about it. She wants him to force his children to be more receptive and treat her in a friendlier, more polite manner. The marital stage is now set for an ongoing battle between the two partners, who have become polarized about the ways in which they should respond to the children's behavior.

Is the parent right to go easy on the children? Is the stepparent right to insist on more deference and more domestic order? The likely situation is that one spouse's style of parenting is much too lax, and the other spouse's style of parenting is appropriately firm but too harsh. The couple can easily fall into painful, irresolvable cycles in which the stepparent sees a stepchild as a "fresh-mouthed, devious little brat" and a biological parent becomes defensive and responds that "she's just a kid," and "Can't you show some understanding of what she has been through?"

Neither the permissive/kind nor the authoritarian/hostile parental style is optimal when it comes to the children's development and growth. There are now a large number of studies demonstrating that children do best on every measure imaginable with authoritative (not authoritarian!) parenting. "Authoritative parents are both loving and firm," explains Papernow:

> They're responsive and attuned to the children. They are caring but they set limits and make developmentally appropriate demands for mature behavior—for instance, "You have every right to be mad about this, but you are old enough to not throw things. You can tell me in *words*." That's authoritative parenting. Permissive parenting is, "Oh, honey, that's all right. If you're bad and make a mess, I understand what you're going through, and it's not a major problem," while authoritarian parenting is, "You must never do that again! You have no right to do that, and it is outrageous!"

It will come as no surprise that a particularly charged issue in remarried systems can be the meting out of discipline, especially given that the members of the couple may have migrated into polarized parenting positions. Therefore, a thorny, frequently quarrelsome issue is this: Does the unrelated stepparent ever have the right to punish the biological parent's child, and if so, under what conditions?

The stepfamily literature is united on this subject, and the answer that it has given is firm and clear: *no,* the stepparent cannot punish the spouse's child. (Sometimes, as shall be seen in the case of the Duvaliers, the rare exception to this rule exists and seems to work well.) By and large, however, it is the biological parent who is empowered to mete out punishments, while the stepparent's role is closer to that of a monitor, a nanny, an aunt, or a babysitter—someone who is in charge while the blood-related parent is absent but is in no way entitled to punish the child's misbehavior. The stepparent reports to the biological parent, "I think that Laura is falling back on her homework, and she's also picking on her sister unmercifully," and the parent decides on the consequences that the child's behavior merits.

As the mother of three spirited daughters, I have always looked at this stepparental stricture as somewhat unrealistic. Many worrisome or obnoxious kid behaviors seem to me to demand more than a delayed response. When I said so to Papernow, she shook her head and said that all of the research findings—and her own experience—were in accord on this point. The stepparent can face up to the children in an authoritative manner but is never the one who can set their punishments.

"Suppose I am the stepparent and my husband is away on a business trip," I asked Papernow, "and I walk into his ten-year-old son's room and find him glued to his small TV, and I know he hasn't touched his school assignments for the next day? What do I do? Do I say, 'You haven't done your homework yet, so the television has to go off immediately?'"

"That's exactly what you say," she replied.

"Suppose he gets lippy and says his favorite TV show is about to come on, and it's none of my business anyway—I'm not his mom! And he can do his homework anytime he wants at his mother's house!"

Papernow smiled, said that then you take a long, deep breath and try to keep your body in a state of neutral arousal. After that you say, as calmly as you can, "I know I'm not your mom. You have a mom, and you're free to follow her rules when you're in her house. But I am the adult in charge here, and we both know the rule of this house is *No TV before homework.* This is a situation for your dad to handle, and he is the one who will handle it. I'll talk about it with him when I speak to him later on tonight."

The rule of thumb is that before the biological parent leaves, he or she tells the children that the stepparent is the person in authority, like an aunt or a babysitter, and she or he enforces the rules of the house. (This temporary transfer of power had, of course, never happened in the Albright family, where Gabe was being given the message that Julie's requests could be discounted.) Generally speaking, though, when it comes to punishments—grounding, loss of allowance—the natural parent is the person in charge of discipline.

Here it must be emphasized that the remarried couple's true underlying dilemma is that often the biological parent does need to firm up and the stepparent does need to show more patience and compassion. If the pair is already polarizing, the stepparent might be saying to the partner, "You're behaving like a wimp, letting that manipulative brat twist you around his finger!"

This is a full-scale attack, to which the biological parent might counter, "You're being so harsh to him, no wonder he's resistant and won't listen to you!" Obviously what follows will be a non-negotiable argument rather than a conversation about an ongoing problem. The couple needs to learn how to communicate in a way that is respectful and caring. I suggest some helpful conversational coping mechanisms in the section below on interpersonal skills.

Challenge Four: Cultural Collisions

As the Blakeslees exemplify, first-time families get started at a time when the married couple's shared culture is already somewhat formed, and their family civilization continues to grow and amplify as each new child comes along. The point too often overlooked is the radically different ways in which remarried families begin. In this instance, the new family gets started with a strong set of cultural givens that are shared by the biological parent and the children. Or if both husband and wife bring children to the marriage, there are two sets of cultural agreements between the parent/child units (the so-called complex family), one of which will usually become more dominant. The vital issue here is that the cultural common ground—the accustomed rhythms of daily life—is *not* that which has been agreed upon by the newly re-wedded adult couple but by the single parent and his or her own mini-family.

There are foregone conclusions between the single parent and the children about commonplace matters, such as: What is a loud voice? Where do you put your coat when you come into the house? Do you do the dishes as soon as dinner is over, or do you relax and leave them in the sink until much later in the evening? What is a reasonable amount to pay for a pair of sneakers? and so forth. The answers to a host of such trivial-seeming questions may be obvious to the biologically bonded members of the family, but they can raise the hackles of the newcomer to the group. Indeed, one ongoing argument between Julie and Matt Albright involved the spectacularly large amounts Matt's son was allowed to spend on his clothing. Julie thought it ridiculous to allow a twelve-year-old to plunk down two hundred dollars on a polo shirt. "He's a *kid!*" she'd objected, scandalized. "He is *my* kid!" Matt had growled. "And as long as I have the money, he is welcome to spend it!"

Differences about money often become a freighted issue in remarried families, and Papernow's preferred strategy for finessing these problems is known as the three-pot solution. Couples who work out this form of compromise keep three separate accounts instead of pooling their finances in the interest of rapid blending. One account is held jointly by the two partners, and is used for running the household—repairs, food bills, and the like. Another account contains the wife's savings, her earnings, and her child support, and this is used for her own expenses and those of her children. A separate and third account is maintained by the husband, and this is designated for his private expenses and those of his children. However, it must be said that there are many subtle intricacies when it comes to money and remarriage, and these are explored in greater detail in chapter 7.

Varying tastes in food can also be a problematic issue in remarrying systems, as they were for another family I interviewed. In this case, the wife and her thirteen-year-old daughter ate fish, chicken, vegetables, brown rice, and no desserts other than sorbets or fruit. They were watching their weight continually and avoided carbohydrates. Her new spouse and his ten-year-old son and eight-year-old daughter were meat and potato eaters and were used to finishing up their dinners with something rich and chocolaty.

When couples remarry, there are a number of such unpredictable differences that will require renegotiation. They may be small or not so small. Does the family that the newcomer is joining simply throw the silverware in the drawer without separating it, or do they put the knives, forks, and spoons in their separate dividers? What are the rules about television and those about homework? If there are teenagers at home, what is the attitude about curfew? "If, for example, a family with a two a.m. curfew for their teenaged children joins up with a family with an eleven p.m. curfew for their teens, how is the couple to handle it?" asked Papernow rhetorically. Then she answered her own question. "This is something that truly matters, so you compromise. It probably becomes a midnight curfew for everyone."

As the remarriage gets underway, a host of unexpected issues are suddenly up for discussion, and the opportunities for disappointment and hurt feelings are legendary. The underlying challenge here—and it is a big one—is that the adult couple charged with managing the negotiation about the mores of daily life is constantly divided by stepfamily architecture, which tends to create stuck outsiders and stuck insiders within a relatively rigid family system. The new couple has been afforded almost no time in which to work out their own differences, agreements, and easy pathways to action. Their relationship is in the process of formation, and their common ground is still very thin. Psychoeducation alone—an understanding of the nature of the complex structure within which they are operating—can often bring a remarkable sense of relief.

According to Papernow, there are some situations in which it may be the better part of wisdom to leave a few irritating differences in place until matters sort themselves out. "You have to focus only on what is vitally important—safety, civility—and you also have to reassure the youngsters about what familiar parts of their routine are going to stay the same. Because these kids have had to live through so many disorienting upheavals already."

Challenge Five: The Other Parent

Although it is well established that battling ex-spouses have a negative impact upon their offspring's later adjustment, it is also true that the divorced mates can sometimes be inappropriately cozy. A single husband may be having chatty evening discussions with his ex-wife during which they talk over the day's events and their mutual children's scheduling. However, once a stepparent enters the scene, a boundary must be drawn around the new relationship.

Papernow's helpful suggestion is that a "Dutch door" should be erected between the former relationship and the new marriage: "The top half remains open to facilitate issues and schedules relating to the children. But the bottom half now needs to close, providing a clear barrier in regard to personal issues and personal time," she said.

It occurred to me that no such Dutch door had been created around Julie and Matthew Albright's remarriage. Matt's first wife, Fran, had remained an integral part of the domestic scene, phoning him when she needed small repairs of any kind and telling him that she still loved him. And significantly, Fran and Matt had joined up in criticizing Julie's parenting, thereby suggesting that their son owed no respect to his stepmother even during the many occasions when she was the sole adult in charge of his care. It was clear that Matt's first marriage had not really ended when his second one began.

Far more commonplace are those situations in which strained relations between first- and later-married households quickly develop. In the happily remarried Duvalier family, for example, the remarried partners were continually plagued by weekly dramas staged by Cliff's ex-wife. Lorraine would never permit a change in the custodial schedule unless she changed the schedule herself, and then she might do so without any forewarning.

Sara Duvalier had tried in vain to make peace with this difficult woman, but that had proven impossible. Nevertheless, the Duvaliers were close allies as far as dealing with these ongoing difficulties was concerned. And very wisely, when Cliff's children returned from their mother's house and declared that she was "crazy," Sara never succumbed to the temptation to join them in bad-mouthing her. Instead, she had focused compassionately on the youngsters' feelings while remaining calm, receptive, and attuned to them in their distress.

What of the fact that the children frequently rotate from one home to the other, and there will be different folkways in the houses of the biological parent and the remarried couple? For instance, if Anne and Bill Blakeslee's children are allowed to have Coke at their mom's house, doesn't that oblige Anne and Bill to permit them to do so also? Why should Anne and Bill insist they drink only milk?

In this very common instance, Patricia Papernow has a helpful metaphor for the new partners to offer the children of divorce and remarriage: "Having two houses, like Mom's house and Dad's house, is like having two different teachers, Mrs. Smith and Mr. Jones. In Mrs. Smith's class you have to raise your hand even to sharpen your pencil. In Mr. Jones' class you can walk around anytime." This low-key, sensible explanation enables the adults in the differing households to adhere to their own ways of being without implying that one is better than the other. Like the two teachers' classes, their homes are simply run differently, and that is perfectly acceptable.

Interpersonal Skills

When learning about and discussing the five challenges—that is, psychoeducation—isn't enough, the couple often needs to go a step further and learn more skillful ways of addressing one another. For example, in the parenting tasks discussion above, the stepmother had called her husband a "spineless wimp" for not coming down harder on his recalcitrant son, and the dad spat back, claiming that his wife was so harsh and uncompassionate that it was little wonder that the boy wouldn't listen to her! The pair had retreated to opposite sides of the boxing ring, and neither was hearing anything the other was saying.

How might this loaded conversation have gone differently?

One means of approaching it is known as the "soft-hard-soft" method. This ingenious technique, devised by Papernow, involves wrapping a highly sensitive message like a sandwich inside two caring, understanding statements—one of which precedes and one of which follows its problematic filling. Soft-hard-soft is a targeted skill designed to aid the couple in their dealings with hypersensitive parenting and stepparenting issues.

How might that sound in the instance just cited? It could start out with something friendly, loving, and understanding. The stepparent might say, "I know this is a confusing transition for Timmy, and you are doing your best to help him keep up with his grades and schoolwork. But when you're not here, he sees it as a chance to test my authority and flout the rules about homework and TV. I know you want him to do well, and I think he's basically a good kid. So can we talk about this? How can we handle this? How can we let him know I'm in charge when you're away and that if he disobeys repeatedly, you will follow up with real consequences? What's your feeling about this?"

With a soft opening along these lines, a hard message in the middle, and a soft ending to the inquiry, the couple would be far more likely to get in a heart-to-heart discussion rather than into a bitter, name-calling argument.

Another helpful skill has to do with letting go of "you" messages and replacing them with "I" messages. A statement such as, "Your daughter came in last night and left crackers and cheese strewn all over the sideboard. She acts like she was raised in a barn!" is highly likely to raise defensiveness and resentment on the part of the parent. Consider instead this "I" message: "It's hard for me when I come down in the morning and find the kitchen in so much disorder," or, "I have a hard time with Emma leaving food out after she snacks in the evening; I'm worried about spoilage, and I also worry about mice." "I" messages are far less accusatory in tone.

The key here is to phrase sentences as appeals rather than as criticisms: "I'd be really happy if you hung up the towels after your morning showers," or "Messes in the kitchen are tough for me. I'd love it if we could work on keeping the counters clean" are two good examples of this approach.

We know that a multitude of differences are likely to pop up in remarriage situations, so it is essential to assume a posture of curiosity about the other members of the household rather than to view disparities as personal offenses. Suppose, for instance, that Bill Blakeslee's new wife, Anne, decides to bake her favorite chocolate cake when her husband's girls are coming over for Italian Night. It is meant to be a surprise for the children, but Bill's younger daughter, Susie, gets upset and bursts into tears when Anne brings it to the table. What Anne didn't know is that Susie *adores* chocolate, but it invariably gives her a bad case of hives. Instead of snapping at Bill, "You could have warned me about that!" his new wife would be advised to turn to Susie and say thoughtfully, "So you're allergic to chocolate? Gee, I didn't know that about you. Let's see what else we can find in the fridge for your dessert. I think we have ice cream and some nice berries." Taking a deep breath and maintaining an attitude of "learning about Susie" is a constructive way of remaining emotionally connected while dealing with inevitable mishaps of this sort.

Psychic Bruises in Bad Places

When psychoeducation and improved interpersonal skills have not produced significant progress and the couple feels stuck, forces at the deepest level of the remarriage structure are likely to be at play. Suppose that Bill Blakeslee's second wife, Anne, grew up in a family where she felt neglected and her needs went unattended due to an older sibling's illness. Because she is sensitized to the experience of being discounted, she's likely to be devastated if Bill's older daughter, Laura, addresses her only in curt monosyllables and consistently avoids eye contact. Being overlooked and ignored in this way opens old wounds, and this is something that Anne finds intolerable—though she herself may never make the connection between her distant past and what's happening in the present.

In remarriage situations, a new husband or wife walks into a family culture that is ready-made, one that he or she has had no part in creating. I can recall a situation in which a lawyer with three daughters (his wife had custody) married a second wife with one son, age twelve. This man was an extremely orderly person, and in his first marriage, his spouse had kept a spotless, smoothly running home. But his new mate and her son were very relaxed about the housekeeping, and the meals were not always ready on time—if they were ready at all. Their cleanup standards were also very different from his own—something that had charmed him initially but became extremely disturbing. This individual required a course of therapy before making the link between his present circumstances and the somewhat chaotic, disorganized family in which he had grown up.

In short, psychic bruises in bad places typically involve situations in which a person's painful experiences in his or her family of origin invade the here-and-now of present-day remarried life. Papernow offers a crisp explanatory example. If you hit your arm in a bad place, you say "ouch!" because it hurts, but if you've hit yourself in a place that is already bruised, it can hurt in a very different way. And if that bruise is a very deep one—one that you may not even be consciously aware of—just touching it may unleash feelings that are simply intolerable.

What to do? When someone in the new family is constantly being triggered by old bruises and reacting in ways that are out of all proportion, it may be useful to begin reflecting upon one of the following questions:

"In the family in which I grew up, who were the insiders and the outsiders?"

"In my family of origin, how did each of my parents treat me?"

"How were differences and disagreements handled?"

"In what ways do the seemingly overblown reactions I'm now having make sense in light of my experiences in the family in which I grew up?"

Still other questions for self-reflection might be:

"Why do I feel so frantic when my spouse gets completely absorbed in her daughter?"

"Why do I feel so consumed with rage when my stepson comes home and greets his mom but doesn't even say hello to me?"

"What happens inside me when my husband fails to deal firmly with his kids' inappropriate behavior?"

In some fortunate instances, the particular bruise that is being activated in the remarried family can be sorted out in quiet discussions with an unusually wise, calm, and empathic partner. However, when it comes to the deep work of disentangling the past from the present, it is far more likely that some therapeutic intervention will be required.

CHAPTER THREE

A New Life:
Sara and Cliff Duvalier,
2009–2010

There is a second pervasive remarital fantasy, closely connected to the myth of instant love, known as the myth of the recreated nuclear family. This is the illusion that the first-marriage family, which has been disrupted in childhood by a parent's death or divorce, will by virtue of the remarriage be restored to its former two-parent nuclear-family status once again.

This widespread myth often goes a giant step further. It not only supports the belief that the formerly intact family will be restored—with the help of the new, more wisely chosen mate—but that the first-time family that was lost can be recreated in a new and vastly improved version. The remarrying couple's rosy-tinted expectation is that the new union will heal the hurts that have been suffered and exorcise any lingering ghosts of the past. The grand goal that the new partners have in mind is the swift creation of the joyful family each had been hoping for in the first place. They seem to believe it possible to stir up some sort of family concentrate using new ingredients and produce an immediately integrated, thriving household. But things rarely proceed according to this plan.

First of all, it flies in the face of biology and plain common sense, for two of the people in the new family—the remarried partners—share an intimate, romantic involvement. Their relationship has a history too, however brief that history may be—such as the shine they took to each other when they met at a friend's home; the picnic they shared after climbing a mountain; the wonderful play they saw and the romantic dinner they enjoyed afterward; and so forth. But if one or both mates are bringing children from their former marriages into the newly forming household, there are clearly junior members of the family who have only the sketchiest of shared memories and little real connection with the stranger/stepparent who has come to inhabit their household.

Moreover, the new wife and mother, now a stepparent, shares a deep biological bond and a long family history with her own offspring. She obviously knows her spouse's children much less well; her attachment to them is still in the process of forming. The husband and dad, a new stepparent, is in a similar position: at the outset of the remarriage he has a relatively superficial knowledge of his partner's children and a much older, far more intense attachment to his own. Yet here they all are, living in the closest proximity.

Second, and of equal (if unarticulated) importance, is the fact that the new family often comes into existence burdened by deeply irrational pressures, such as the powerfully felt need to have the remarriage make up for the losses and disappointments experienced earlier. Thus, the first difficulties that remarrying pairs are likely to confront are created by these underlying fault lines and the inevitable disappointments posed by their own wildly unrealistic expectations. It is considerations such as these that have given rise to a remarriage literature full of cautions and warnings, advising the new partners that they can anticipate a host of unnerving shocks and difficulties.

As Wednesday Martin writes in her cautionary work for presumptive stepmothers, *Stepmonsters,* "You [the stepparent] are entering into a web of habits, preferences, inside jokes, problems, hopes, rituals, and history that precedes you and very likely excludes you." The "sensation of being an outsider, a feeling that things are set up to preclude intimacy, particularly in the first one to three years of a partnership" is viewed as a given by this author, who sees the cards of the new relationship as stacked against the remarrying newcomer.

However, in my own experience, things don't always proceed in this negative fashion. In the course of my many interviews with remarried partners, I have met with a number of couples who seem to have integrated their former family cultures with surprisingly minimal difficulties. Although certain challenges have arisen along the way, these partners have managed to establish a solid base in which their newly formed civilization is experienced as whole and nourishing, and its members have the comfortable feeling of being included. They have become insiders.

What factors set these more fortunate mates apart? My own sense is that the important element that underlies their success is their own eyes-wide-open, realistic expectations in regard to what remarried life will be like and their mature interpersonal skills in terms of their ability to comfortably negotiate the glitches and misunderstandings that are inevitable in remarriage systems.

LUCKY TO BE LEFT

The Duvaliers, who had seven children between them when they remarried—four were Sara's and three were Cliff's—were in the fourth year of their new marriage when I interviewed them. It was a second marriage following divorce for both of them. During our first interview, I asked Sara to complete the following sentence: "A myth that people seem to perpetuate about remarriage is . . . what?" I waited, gazing at her questioningly.

Sara, in her midforties, friendly and vivacious, shook her short blond hair. She didn't hesitate long before responding, "A myth about remarriage? It's that they are doomed to fail. I hear that so often."

I nodded and said that a lot actually do.

She was a quiet for a moment, then said thoughtfully, "I think I can speak for both of us when I say we believe there are two kinds of people. There are those who marry with the idea of staying with that one partner, and there are those who are always looking around for a different, better option. Neither one of us is that second kind of person, which may explain why we stayed in those not-good relationships as long as we did." She blushed slightly, then said, "I can't imagine myself being strong enough to have come out and said, 'I'm leaving you because you are so mean and such a bully and such a—a *jerk*.'"

"So you were lucky you got left," I said, for I had already learned that Tom, her ex-husband, had walked out on her and their four children when their youngest was just ten.

"I am *so* lucky I was left." The words came out in one rushing, grateful breath. I took that to mean that she'd never have had the courage to do the leaving, no matter how bad things had become.

Cliff touched his wife's shoulder lightly, "Both of us are. In retrospect, my situation is pretty much the same thing."

"Did Lorraine leave you as well?" There had already been some discussion of Cliff's difficult ex-wife, but I'd never asked him that specific question.

He didn't answer directly. "We had problems, but I was always thinking that if we did this thing or that thing, then things were going to be better. But yes, she left. She had an affair, and that felt right to her. The man was a doctor—he was married too, but that was no problem. They rearranged their lives and waltzed off, and I—I'm sitting there shocked and hurt, emotionally drained." Cliff's strong, deep voice, cracked momentarily. "But you come out of something like that and you go 'Whooosh,' it's over, and I'm in one piece, and it's not that bad."

I smiled. "So then, answer the question that Sara just answered. 'A myth that people seem to perpetuate about remarriage is . . . ?'"

"Is that they are doomed to failure. They're *not*." The Duvaliers turned to one another and exchanged a long, affectionate look.

"Obviously you two found yourself in a different, much better place," I said.

Sara nodded and said that was why they were both so excited about taking part in my study. She believed that many people had a negative view of remarriage, and she and her husband wanted to tell their story as a positive and supportive one. I looked at Cliff, a tall, well-built man of fifty-three with a head of light-brown hair. He was nodding his agreement, snatching glances at Sara all the meanwhile.

I paused, thinking about the remarriage books and papers I had been reading, many of them replete with descriptions of the inevitable shocks, disappointments, disillusionments, and breakdowns that litter the road to the yearned-for remarital success.

Then I smiled, told them that they were not the only couples with positive stories to tell.

"I have seen folks who, like you two, came from long, dreadful marriages and remarried happily later on in their lives," I said, then added, "Of course, I've seen plenty of the opposite as well."

Cliff leaned forward in his seat, said earnestly that people like that hadn't really done the preparatory work in advance. "They haven't said 'All right, this is how we are going to handle our combined family.' Instead, from the get-go, they split them down the middle. One parent is disciplining her kids and one person is disciplining his kids—and that's where the great divide is, as far as I'm concerned."

I was surprised, for as far as discipline is concerned, most remarriage experts *do* advise this particular strategy—that is, leaving discipline to the biological parent. The stepparent is usually cautioned against stepping into what can easily become family quicksand. Instead, he or she is advised to act as a sympathetic consultant and monitor of the child's behavior while leaving it to the blood-related parent to take the reins when the rules of behavior need to be reinforced. The purpose is to avoid falling into the role of "step-ogre" or confronting a stonewalling child who says, "You can't tell me what to do! You're not my mom [or dad]!"

"How do you two handle discipline?" I inquired.

This time it was Sara who replied. "The way we do it is that we have house rules," she said promptly. "So everything happens in the ways *we* say it has to be. When Cliff first moved into our home after our marriage, I wanted to be the one to discipline my kids. I was afraid my wild boys would be too much." She shrugged. "But it's ridiculous. You can't have somebody living with you who has no say—it's actually an insult to that person. So we talked it over, and we never did do it that way. We do everything together."

She gave me a long, appraising look, as if expecting me to disapprove of or disbelieve in this tactic. "Truly," she said.

A BRIEF ASIDE: WHERE TO LIVE?

Sara had mentioned that Cliff had moved into her home, which meant that he had entered as an outsider to the rhythms of her daily life—the ways the space was used; where the silverware and linen were stored; where the TV was and how much it was on; and other rules, regulations, and tacit understandings of her family culture.

Obviously Sara and her children were immersed in this culture, and any changes Cliff desired would have to be negotiated. Theoretically, she might have been open to change but found it hard on herself—or on one or more of her children—when her new spouse wanted some aspects of their lives to be different (for example, how often the TV was on). It could have even felt like an intrusion when Cliff wanted to rearrange some of the furniture.

Some remarriage experts say that when financial resources are available, a new house equalizes insider and outsider pressures for everyone. In this instance, such a move would have meant a big change for Sara's children, and it is known that when the velocity of change goes up, the well-being of the youngsters involved goes down. So it was easier to have Cliff move into Sara's home. In this circumstance, things go best when the insider parent is attuned to both her children's need for stability *and* the new spouse's need to make the changes that will make him feel at home and comfortable.

Cliff was a nonresidential parent, with three high-school-age children of his own. His kids came to his new home for brief visits and were therefore outsiders to Sara's family's rules and habits. When things go well, as they appeared to be doing for the Duvaliers, the new partners are attuned to how hard this is for the outsider child or children—and also for the children who are in their home and may feel intruded upon. The partners are empathic and caring of both "home" children and "visitor" children. Remarriage experts say that it is always helpful for the visiting children to have some designated space—a dresser, a side of a bedroom— that is theirs and belongs to them alone.

THURSDAY NIGHTS ARE GREAT NIGHTS

I asked Sara whether they, like some other remarried partners I'd interviewed, had house rules posted on a cork board or on the refrigerator. Sara giggled and turned to Cliff. "I suppose we do . . . they seem to come down, but sometimes we re-post them." They both laughed, and Sara turned back to me. "My kids know that if they ask Cliff a question and he gives an answer, that's the answer I am going to give. And we talk that answer over first. We're really pretty easygoing, but there are definite limits," she said in a good-natured tone of voice.

I asked them if little things like whether the children hung up their coats when they came in or threw them over the back of a chair were ever points of contention. "Things like that—little things—happen in different ways in different families," I probed.

Cliff grinned, "Our kids never pick up. Wet towels, sneakers, shoes, coats, books, backpacks, dishes . . ." Both he and Sara started laughing again.

"I mean, our house is clean," she reassured me, "because I'm running around chasing them, or Cliff is running around chasing after them. But we are sticklers on certain things—such as that nobody can start eating until everybody sits down. That was a *huge* rule of ours that took forever to get set in their minds." She paused, as if trying to think of another of the household regulations.

Cliff then said, "Yes, and family dinner night is Thursday night. So all our kids, Sara's and mine, come together for that meal."

I asked him if that was his night to have custody, and he nodded; that particular weekday night and every other weekend were the times his children came to their home. "Thursday night is a great night, because everybody knows they shouldn't be making other plans. It's looser in the summertime, but during the school year, they all know that unless it's a sports event, that's our night together," he told me.

"So you two do manage to create house rules," I said, thoughtfully. "But what happens if somebody breaks the rules. Are there consequences?"

Sara nodded. "Yes, there are. My daughter drank when she was in tenth grade—she took a shot, or something. So we had her write a paper on what's important in life and on making the right friends, and we also grounded her for two weeks." She stopped and grinned, then turned to Cliff, who started to laugh. "You're laughing," she said, then turned to me. "Cliff works from home, so he was stuck with her the whole time, but actually, my daughter has an extremely close relationship with Cliff. She's close to her dad too, so she has things pretty well figured out."

"You don't think she will make the same mistake in judgment that you originally made?" I asked, for Sara's husband had been flagrantly unfaithful almost from the outset and ultimately walked out on his wife and children with his latest mistress.

"I *am* concerned about that, for her," said Sara soberly. "She's cute, she's smart, very energetic. But she always goes for the boy who is . . . I don't know . . . not really that nice to her. So she is a work in progress. Actually we both worry."

"Yes," said Cliff empathically, moving closer and placing his hand lightly around his wife's shoulder.

I THOUGHT I COULD SHOW HIM
HOW TO BE HAPPY

Sara had married her first husband at age twenty-one, after what sounded like a delightful, unclouded childhood in a countrified suburb in Connecticut. The home that her family lived in had been built by her father, and it included an extra wing that was occupied by her beloved grandparents after her granddad's retirement. She had one sibling, a younger brother, to whom she remained close, and two dear aunts—her father's sisters—whose families lived nearby, in the New York/Long Island area. "We spent every holiday and every summer together, always. So we cousins are close even now. They are more like siblings," she said warmly.

It sounded like a wonderful family to come from, I thought—not the kind that seems to be the logical prelude to a punishing, disrespectful, ultimately failed eighteen-year marital relationship. I asked Sara to complete the following sentence: "My first marriage could be described as . . . ?"

"A challenging learning experience," she replied tersely, and I asked her to fill in the blanks.

She inhaled deeply, then let out the breath with a sigh. "We got married six weeks after I graduated from college, so I was obviously very young. And I think my ex-husband, whom I'd known since age eighteen, was not a very happy person ever. I guess I really wanted to show him how nice life could be. I would bring him into all of this, my big, happy family, and he could be a part of it and life could be great, but I came to realize our views are so extremely different. I have the glass-half-full approach, and he always has the glass half empty. This meant he was never satisfied—not in our marriage, not with anything. He was always searching for something—more money, more things, more everything."

During the first years of their marriage, the couple had lived in Germany, where Tom was serving with the Reserve Officers' Training Corps. She considered that to have been a good way to start a marriage, because they were separated from their families and had to work things out on their own. "I mean, the two of us were in Germany. But Tom has an aggressive energy about him. He *looks* like a military person. And I was always trying to buffer things around him, to placate him, soften the edges, keep him happy. But in the long run, inevitably, that doesn't work. He had an affair." The look on her face was stricken.

"He had an affair." I repeated her own words quietly.

She nodded her head yes, and said that he had actually had two affairs that she knew of—the second one lasting for a whole year, with a young woman of nineteen. They had been back in Connecticut at that time. "I was young myself. I was only twenty-seven, and we had four little ones, and he had this long-term affair." She had discovered it when she picked up the phone to make a call and heard him talking to his lover. At first he'd insisted that he'd only slept with this young woman one time, but eventually the whole truth emerged.

"What still bothers me is that he never did apologize, never said he was sorry about that affair," Sara said, looking baffled. It was as if she were still surprised not only by her ex-spouse's behavior but by his lack of guilt.

At that time, they had been living near her family, but in the wake of the marital crisis that ensued, they moved to another part of Connecticut. "We wanted to make a fresh start, so we relocated to a town near New Haven—to a sweet old house in Woodbridge, Connecticut." She paused, shrugged her shoulders as if to indicate, "What else could you expect," and then said that in the course of time, the same thing had happened: he'd had another affair. "Again I found out by mistakenly picking up the phone. Foolish me," Sara said wryly, then added in a frightened tone of voice, "This time he left."

AN ONGOING, DAMAGING INFLUENCE

While Sara attributed her foolish choice of mate to the fact that she had married at the age of twenty-one, Cliff hadn't married until he was in his early thirties, and he described that twelve-year marriage as a "disaster" almost from the very beginning. I asked him to fill me in on what he meant and what had gone wrong. "We were just two people who, personality-wise, values-wise, could probably never have made it in the long run. There wasn't a common platform that we shared, emotionally, intellectually . . ." His voice trailed off.

I asked him to tell me more about his ex-wife. "Lorraine is more than just difficult. She's a step further out—she's got psychological issues," he replied. He said nothing further, so I asked him if he believed that she suffered from depression.

Cliff shook his head. "It's more along the lines of what's called 'borderline personality disorder,' if I was going to pick out a diagnosis." That particular mental complaint comes with such a grab bag of different descriptions that I asked him if he could give me a specific instance of what he meant.

Cliff turned to Sara, "Can you think of an example?"

"Yes, the rotten way she left you." She turned to me, said,

"Lorraine had an affair, a long-term one, with a close friend of theirs—which I think is so *mean*. She tells lies all the time and is extremely manipulative. Just learning how to deal with her is so difficult, because she cycles through people and she really has no friends. Actually, Cliff and I had to go to therapy just to learn how to deal with her."

Cliff laughed a short barking sound. "There isn't a week that goes by that there is not another chapter in the serial drama." Sara, looking perturbed, said that they really didn't want to spend their whole time with me discussing his ex-wife, but the truth was that they did have to deal with her on a daily basis. I smiled and asked Cliff to describe the most recent chapter of Lorraine's ongoing intrusions.

Again he hesitated, as if at a loss to describe the clouds of confusion and agitation that his ex-wife managed to arouse. Then he said, speaking carefully and slowly, that she had eventually married her lover, and the two of them would go on vacations quite often. "On the one hand, she doesn't consider me a 'fit parent,' so the kids can only come here on visitation times—Thursdays and every other weekend. Literally."

"Though they're now seventeen, sixteen, and fourteen," put in Sara. "They live just a few miles away, and they would love to spend more time here."

"On the other hand, if she wants to go on vacation—and we can go into details ad nauseam on her India trip—then the whole 'fit parent' thing flips over, and she becomes quite threatening about letting us know that we *must* take the kids while she's away. As a matter of fact, if we should get an e-mail today, the deadline would be tomorrow for us to agree that we would take the kids."

"We would actually love to take them any time," explained Sara. "It's just that we want her to let them come over whenever they want to—not just on visitation days and when she wants to go on vacation."

"She's decided that's not going to happen, no way. And she just pops over here, and she'll be working on some other contentious kind of scheme," said Cliff grimly. Sara placed a calming hand on his knee, said, "I think the happier we are, the more angry she gets. Because she's not completely happy, so the situation keeps getting more intense."

I asked them if the therapist they'd consulted about this situation had been helpful, and both nodded. "Oh yes," said Sara. "She explained to us—mostly to me, because I was new on the scene—that Cliff's ex-wife would never change. She told me that whatever I might do—no matter what strategy I tried—her behavior would be what it is, and the way it will be until she dies. So I could either deal with it or leave the relationship; that was it. I didn't have any other choice. Which to me was kind of freeing. I realized that I could be nice to her, try to accommodate her, but she would never change. So it's just something that we manage. The enormity of the problem went away, because whatever issue we were having at that time, I realized . . ." Her voice trailed off.

"You knew you couldn't change it," I completed her sentence.

Cliff leaned forward, said, "Even if Sara reached out and tried to be nice—as she did do initially—then Lorraine would try to work her way into our existence and do her damage. She is just a damaging person. So there's just very little communication—the minimum possible—at this point."

This was still hard on them as parents, said Sara, because Cliff's three kids were still at the center of the ongoing turmoil. The anxiety and distress in her voice made it sound as if she were speaking not of her husband's children but her own.

THE EX-WIFE SYNDROME

As Sandra Kahn notes in *The Ex-Wife Syndrome,* there are two major ways in which ex-spouses can remain "married" to husbands they have seemingly left behind years earlier. These avenues may look very different from the outside, but their underlying purpose is the same: to retain a live-wire connection to a marriage bond that has long since been legally severed.

One way is to remain emotionally dependent on the ex-spouse, as Matthew Albright's former wife had done. Not only did Fran form an intense friendship with Matthew's new wife, Julie, but she had managed to remain Gabe's only "real" parent, even though Julie often found herself in the role of the caregiver. Fran had even made that sentimental phone call on the anniversary of their first meeting to let her ex-husband know he was still the main man in her life. She didn't sever the cord of that first marriage until many years later. Kahn calls this way of remaining emotionally stuck in a lost relationship the "bondage of caring."

The other means of staying rooted in an extinct marriage is one that Kahn calls the "bondage of bitterness"—and the weekly dramas initiated by Cliff's ex-wife indicated that she had gone in this direction. Sara believed that although she had eventually married her lover, Lorraine's unhappiness was incurable. "She has no social life. She runs through people, and something always happens—it doesn't work out," she said, adding that the impact of these episodes was the biggest problem that the pair of them had to deal with.

What was at the root of Lorraine's hostile incursions into the Duvaliers' clearly contented, well-functioning household? A person who feels good about herself, who is self-confident and emotionally secure, rarely feels the need to sow dissension and bad feeling in the ways that Cliff's ex-spouse was doing. But Sara had mentioned that the happier she and Cliff seemed to be, the angrier Lorraine became. As Kahn writes, "[Women] whose connection to the ex-husband is dominated by anger and jealousy are often *consumed* by the fight. . . . Jealousy is based on the intense desire to keep something considered personal property from being taken away by another person."

Lorraine had left behind her a man who was damaged and distraught; now she was being confronted with an ex-spouse who was whole and obviously elated by his marriage to his new wife, Sara. I suspected that her frequent assaults on the Duvaliers' household had to do with Kahn's so-called bondage of bitterness. Although Lorraine was the one who had initially left her first marriage, she'd supposed that Cliff (in some dark place in her spirit, still *her* property) would grieve for her forever. His current happiness—and his clear-cut indifference to herself—were developments that she appeared to find deeply insulting and enraging.

WHY DID I STAY?

Sara had described her first marriage as a "challenging learning experience." I asked her what she had learned.

She frowned, said, "I learned a lot about me, because I said to myself afterward, 'Why did I stay so long?'" I glanced down at my notes, reminding myself that she had been wed to her hurtful, betraying spouse for a full eighteen years. "And why were my expectations so low?" she added in a quiet, embarrassed tone.

I waited to hear how she had answered this question for herself, but no such answer was forthcoming. So I ventured to ask if many of her female peers in her high school and college years had been women who were easily put down by men.

Sara shook her head decisively. "No, it's mostly that . . ." She left that sentence unfinished, then began a new one. "If you were to ask my mother or my grandmother about marriage and what makes it successful, it's really the woman: she does most of the placating and smoothing out in order to make things go well. Now my dad is very—mind you, I love my dad!—but he's a very passionate guy. So sometimes he yells and sometimes he cries, but it's always drama, drama, drama. And my mother moves along by his side, steadily working to make things okay."

I nodded at her. "So that's what you knew about."

She nodded her agreement. "Yes, and I married someone who was mood cycling, up and down, but not in a life-loving kind of way. Really, Tom was in a depression. But I didn't see that, and I had this model in my mind, which was that the woman had to keep everything going. Both my mom and my grandmother would always say to my brother and me that when you look at marriage, you had to see the big picture. Sometimes it's bad, but other times it's wonderful, and when you hit the bad times, you have to remember the good times. I tried my best to do that, but it doesn't work when your partner isn't interested in doing that with you."

I reflected aloud that her parents must have been shocked when she decided to divorce. "Or were they?" I asked.

Sara smiled and said that her folks still could not handle it. "My mother can barely talk about it, because she's so angry that this man could have left me and his children! I have had to ask her to stop bringing it up, especially since they really do love Cliff. They actually adore him, and all of our children get along so well!"

"It sounds as if the idea of divorce just blows their mind," I said, and Cliff smiled.

"Yes, it's almost as if *they* have been divorced," he said, and Sara laughed aloud. "Really! It's as though my husband had left *them*. They will never get over it."

A ROCK TO LEAN AGAINST

My next question was directed at Cliff: "The major difference between this relationship and my first marriage is . . . what?" He didn't miss a beat before responding, "Oh, this time I got my soul mate."

Sara jumped slightly, as if she'd been poked in the back. She turned to look at him and he leaned over, placed a light kiss on her lips.

"We share everything," he turned back to tell me.

"We do," agreed Sara.

"Emotionally, intellectually, children," he said.

"Everything," echoed Sara. It had been that way from the moment they had met each other; they had felt so connected to each other. "Cliff is so kind. He is such a kind person. When I walk out the door every day, I know that someone is actually thinking about me—wondering when I'm going to come home tonight and worrying about whether I'm okay."

I turned to Cliff again and asked him what his fantasies had been about how this second marriage would differ from his first one. What parts of those fantasies had come true? What parts were very different from what he'd imagined?

He looked puzzled for a moment, then shrugged. "I don't think I had any fantasies in regard to getting married again. I was single for a period of time, and during those years I was focused on my kids. And on my own stuff a bit, trying to get myself back to someone recognizable, so that I could say, 'Oh yes, that's Cliff Duvalier. I knew him. He was a pretty good guy.' So that's where I was, and I really didn't go out on any serious dates. Then I met Sara, and everything changed. Before that, I would have been scared to death of getting into a relationship—into any relationship at all. I wasn't painting a mural in my mind of something great happening. That would have been too much of a leap. It would have been like going from black and white to a palette full of color."

"You were so shaken up by the divorce that you couldn't think of much beyond mending yourself and staying connected to your kids," I said. It was a statement, not a question.

Cliff said yes, there had been such a huge difference between where he was then and where he could ever have dreamed of going. "Probably I was thinking that there wasn't much use in fantasizing or daydreaming or hoping for something better in my life. I guess my thought was, 'Well, I'm never going to find that.'"

"You were never going to find that," I repeated his statement with a smile. "You couldn't even fantasize about a relationship like this one, and yet it's really happened."

"Yes, it's truly happened," he said. He gave Sara's shoulder a squeeze. "In a very short period of time—four years—we've had so many terrific times and we've also had stressful times. And we've worked through those stressful times together."

"Dealing with something that was going on," said Sara at once, "It's not stress between the two of us." The Duvaliers then explained that during the brief number of years they had been together, each of them had lost a job and had been forced to go out and seek a new one. They had been adept at supporting each other during these uncertain periods.

I asked Sara the same question I'd asked Cliff: Which parts of this remarriage were what she'd imagined in advance, and what had turned out to be very different?

Unlike her husband, Sara had expected it to be extremely stressful. "I was always nervous. I have three teenaged boys, so how could I expect another man to come into our home and have them all get along? My sons are so protective of me because they bore a lot of the burden. They were old enough to know exactly what happened and why when Tom picked up and walked out. So I'm just amazed at how easily we transitioned through all of this and how great Cliff is with my kids. I wouldn't have married him if he hadn't liked my children, but the surprise is that it all went so smoothly."

Sara then told me a story about how her oldest son, Frank, then fifteen, had started crying when she told the boys that Cliff would be moving in with them. She'd been taken aback, because the boys seemed to like Cliff and be pleased by the romance. Frank's objection was that the couple wasn't married yet. "I said, 'But we are going to get married,' and he said, 'Okay, but I don't see a ring.' He was nervous that this new person was going to leave."

It was clear that her son feared that the family would be abandoned a second time and that such a loss would be unbearable.

Sara and Cliff had calmed him down by setting up a meeting with the architect who was building an addition to their house that would accommodate the Duvalier children on their days of visitation. This was sufficient evidence that Cliff was reliable and he was here to stay.

I asked Sara what her experience of stepparenting had been like, and she said that it had been terrific. "Cliff had been in a divorce situation for three years when I met his kids, and they were so excited that their dad had a girlfriend! They were so kind and accepting, and it's never been any different. I kept waiting, kept thinking 'Oh, they will resent me, or the girls will be jealous.' But they are wonderful."

She turned to her husband. "Your kids have always been so much more open than mine, I must say."

Cliff said to me, "They love Sara through and through."

"I love them too," said Sara.

"You've got to realize that their mom isn't consistent. She isn't warm and fuzzy. Sara is the epitome of consistent and warm and fuzzy. So it gives them a real rock to lean against."

I could not help but reflect that everything that I was hearing flew in the face of Wednesday Martin's predictions. In her book *Stepmonsters*, Martin asserts that female competition over access to the husband/stepfather is inevitable. "Like money, husbands are a finite resource. There is only one of him, and he has only so much time and energy." Daughters, she says, are especially prone to competing with the stepparent for the lion's share of their remarried dad's attention and affection. "They tend to behave in ways that will shift the new woman in their father's life into an outsider position," she writes.

"Do you feel like an insider or an outsider in this family?" I asked Sara.

"Insider," she responded immediately

I put the same question to Cliff, and he said that he felt like an insider too.

WHEN FORTUNE SMILES

Remarriage had improved the Duvaliers' lives enormously. They had worked hard to bring their two families together in ways that would prevent difficult feelings from emerging. And their brood of children got along, though some were closer than others. As Sara said, "I think their hearts are in it. They try hard. They all want the marriage to be successful—which is interesting, don't you think?"

I did think it was interesting, because the most-respected theoretical approach currently available—Patricia Papernow's architectural model—suggests that in remarried families, insider/outsider issues can be reliably expected to emerge. However, the Duvaliers and their seven children had come together with an almost inexplicable minimum of friction, and I'd interviewed other re-wed partners with similarly benign experiences. These were couples whose only regrets revolved around the many earlier years that had been wasted in painful, hopelessly unworkable relationships.

Why had fortune smiled upon these pairs?

When I talked to Papernow about partners like the Duvaliers who did not seem to fit into her model, she laughed and told me that these were *not* the couples who arrived in a clinician's office in order to solve problems and seek understanding! On the contrary, these flourishing couples are typically people who enter the relationship not only with realistic expectations and seasoned interpersonal skills but with a well-developed ability to empathize with the special difficulties inherent in the other partner's insider/outsider position. In these felicitous instances, both members of the pair proceed to create their new community slowly, with sensitivity and understanding. They are fully aware that all the children involved have suffered a great loss—the splintering of the first family—and should therefore be handled with care.

Another factor underlying this kind of success is that the mates are free of what Papernow terms "psychic bruises in bad places." If, for example, a stepparent has grown up in a family where she felt like an outsider, then she will be that much more likely to overreact to situations in which she feels excluded—for example, if her spouse and his children are reminiscing at length about a delightful trip abroad that took place long before she became part of the family scene.

To be sure, all of the above elements are not necessarily sufficient for an easy transition into remarital harmony. Most critical, according to the stepfamily literature, are the positive feelings of the children involved—to which I might add the personal qualities of the stepparent, the fit of the two families, and a lot of plain old-fashioned good luck.

CHAPTER FOUR

Soft-Hard-Soft:
Owen and Abbie Jamison,
2010

Owen and Abbie Jamison, both in their early sixties, had been married for over ten years at the time of our interviews. These attractive, young-looking partners struck me as living proof of the current saying that sixty is the new forty. Abbie Jamison is trim, auburn-haired, and bubbling with vitality and sociability. Her husband, Owen, is a tall, large bear of a man with pleasant features and dark, wavy hair with a hint of soft gray at the sideburns.

I found Owen somewhat more reserved than his wife and happy to take a back seat to her effusiveness whenever the possibility occurred. So when I asked the couple what had been the greatest surprise they'd encountered upon remarrying, I didn't expect the response to come from him, but it did.

"It was Rob, Abbie's son, who was ten years old when we married. He made no secret of the fact that he detested me and hated having me as his stepfather. He didn't want to live in my home, or go to school in this community, or have anything to do with me. I was badly shaken, I found it very painful," said, Owen, in a low, hurt tone of voice.

"He is very tenderhearted," said Abbie, touching her husband's shoulder. "All his students love him," she added fondly. "He was in no way prepared to have a stepson reject him."

Owen Jamison is a professor on the faculty of Wesleyan University in Middletown, Connecticut. It was a second marriage for both partners, who had remarried in their late forties. I asked Owen if he had brought children of his own into this new family, and he hesitated briefly before telling me that he had two "actual" children and an adopted child. "In other words, I have two sons by my first wife and also an adopted son who is actually my ex-wife's out-of-wedlock child."

His own boys had been nine and ten years old at the time of his divorce, and his adopted son had been thirteen. He had remained single for a considerable period of time after his marriage's breakup, and his children were now young adults in their late twenties and early thirties. His adopted son was married; both other sons were still single. "Are you close to them?" I asked.

"I'm close to them all," responded Owen without hesitation.

I turned to Abbie, "Are you close to them too—or not so close?" I could read the answer in her sudden blush and her facial expression.

"I wouldn't say I'm very close to them. We're friendly," she said carefully. "I'm not distant, but they were grown or almost so when we got together." Owen's youngest son had been starting college at that time, and none of his children had lived with them as a couple after their father's remarriage.

When I asked Owen how long his prior marriage had lasted, he seemed oddly taken aback by this mundane question. At last, as if making an admission, he said, "Twenty years."

Abbie cut in to say, laughingly, "There are two measures, Maggie. One is the actual time, and the other is how long it felt, emotionally speaking,"

I laughed, too, and said to Owen, "Maybe two hundred years?" He smiled and seemed to relax. "That's about right," he said.

I asked him if his sons were also close to their mother.

"No," he said, without further explanation.

"They are not close to their mother but they are close to you. Period?" I pressed him.

"She's kind of nuts," Abbie intervened. This remark was quite familiar to me, for I'd heard it often in the course of my interviews. A divorced ex-spouse was frequently described as a "nut" or a "bitch," while a dead parent was typically a sanctified, transcendently sublime figure.

I asked Owen to tell me a bit more about his first marriage; he shrugged and said uncomfortably, "It was pretty chaotic."

I made a note on my pad, then looked up to meet his gaze directly. "Chaotic. In what way was it chaotic?"

"My first wife enjoyed confrontations and arguing, and I'm not that kind. I'm neither confrontational nor argumentative, but she wanted to get into battles about every aspect of our lives." A note of acrimony had crept into his voice.

"How about raising your children? Did that become a casus belli also?" I asked mildly.

"Everything was, but in reality I did most of the child raising. She was usually off doing her thing. She considered herself a musician." Owen shrugged again, as if dismissing his ex-wife's musical aspirations as ridiculous.

I asked what instrument she played, and he said tersely, "Guitar."

Had she been a hippie? I probed. He shrugged and said that she had been at Woodstock.

"Was she taking drugs?" I asked, and he said, "No, not that I know of. Maybe she was taking prescription drugs, but nothing illegal."

"Was she faithful?" I asked, and to my astonishment Owen paused, looked puzzled. "Hmm," he said at last, "I don't know."

"You don't know," I repeated his words. "Did you think about it?"

"Yes, I did," he replied.

"But you weren't sure. Did you ever try to ask her about it?"

Owen said he hadn't, and I asked why not. "That would have been confrontational," he replied—a remark that gave me pause, for I found it strange. This conversation seemed to be making Abbie nervous, for she stood up suddenly and said she was going to boil some water in order to warm up the tea the three of us were drinking.

"So even though this thought was passing through your mind, you just didn't want to fight," I continued, in her absence. "Did your ex-wife ever accuse *you* of being unfaithful?"

Owen shook his head no; fidelity wasn't the issue in the marriage. "The real issue was the arguments. We were just fighting, fighting, fighting all the time."

THE DECISION TO BAIL OUT

In a strictly legal sense, Abbie's first marriage had lasted almost as long as Owen's had. However, she had been separated from her ex-husband for several years during that time. When I asked her to flesh out the story of that relationship, she told me that on the positive side, she and her husband had shared "deep ties and common interests." But on the darker, more difficult side, he had turned into a control freak. "He wanted things to be done this way, that way, *his* way, even if I didn't agree with his way. He was definitely *not* a nice person to be around," she said, crossing her arms over her chest in a stance of defiance.

She had met her first husband, who was Jewish, on a kibbutz in Israel. I asked if he was a religious man, and Abbie smiled and shook her head. "No, I was raised a Catholic, but I was more Jewish than he was. I was the one who taught my son about the Jewish holidays. Gary had no real interest in any of that. Also," she said, almost as an afterthought, "he was unfaithful."

I decided to put this charged issue to one side for the moment and asked how long they had been married before they'd had a child. It had been thirteen years, Abbie told me. "Were you trying for a long time, before then?" I asked.

She shook her head. "Nope. I went back to school and got my master's in clinical social work. Gary was busy trying to develop his career, which is now an international one, in shipments of produce. Also, there was that long period of time when we were separated."

"Was it infidelity that led to the separation?" I asked, and she nodded, took a sip of her tea, then said, "Yes, and just a sense of real relief, because we were not compatible at all. I was under so much strain, feeling spent. I didn't want to go along with his program, whatever it happened to be at the moment."

"Then was it more an issue of control than infidelity that led to the separation?"

Replacing her cup in the saucer with a clatter, Abbie said thoughtfully, "Yes, probably so. Control was the core issue. It was what was making the relationship unbearable." After a moment, though, she murmured, "Control and his commitment level."

"Meaning?" I prompted.

"Meaning his affairs. I didn't want to put up with that stuff anymore. Anyway, when we got together after a period of living apart, we renegotiated the relationship. It was going to change, supposedly, in a number of specific ways—but it didn't. When it became clear that Gary was just never going to commit to the marriage, I bailed out. And a significant part of that decision had to do with my son, Rob. I said to myself, 'You will never be a good mother to this child.' How could I be, when I wanted to tear his father limb from limb?"

THE DIFFERENCE THIS TIME

Without specifying who should be the one to answer, I asked them both to describe the major difference between this current relationship and the relationships they had left behind. "This one is much more fun," said Abbie, without hesitation. She laughed. "Owen has no interest in controlling anyone. It's not his thing."

"I'd say this relationship is characterized by love," said Owen, his voice deeply serious. I was moved, for this statement of frank emotion was the equivalent of a long, passionate speech from this reticent academic.

I smiled at him and said, "This is a loving relationship—and the other, argumentative relationship was characterized by hostility?" He nodded, said that actually there had been a loving sense at the outset of his first marriage, but it had dissipated fairly rapidly.

Abbie's expression was thoughtful. "Do you have something you want to say?" I asked her, and she nodded. "Oh, just that this relationship really *is* much more fun, but that's not the main deal."

Owen turned to her and said, "I do agree that it is much more fun."

"We're playful," said Abbie. "We do silly things, like dress up in costumes. Last week we went to a costume contest at a party given by one of Owen's ex-students. It was a big bash, and we created these characters. Owen was a Mississippi oil tycoon, and I was his trophy wife. I was dressed up as an elegant cowgirl with a satin blouse and a platinum wig and these killer cowboy boots." They both started laughing. "We did it to win the contest—and we *did*," Abbie told me gaily.

"The first prize was a huge chocolate bar," Owen said, with a grin.

"You two do have a good time," I said, looking from one to the other with a smile.

"We do. So I would say there is definitely love—but also commitment." Abbie's voice had grown thoughtful.

"You don't feel that Owen is looking over your shoulder to see who else is out there?" I asked.

"Never," replied Abbie. "I've never felt that. Also, we have a deep spiritual understanding that we share." The Jamisons had already explained to me that they were both followers of a famous Indian mystic and had met one another years earlier during a pilgrimage to this holy man's ashram in India.

A PRIVATE TALK

I turned to Abbie and asked her the same question I had asked Owen earlier: What had been her greatest surprise following the remarriage? A shadow crossed her features, and she said that she was a sixth-generation Californian; she hadn't realized how painful it would be to move across the country and away from the sunny, warm countryside in which she'd grown up. Also, she'd felt acutely homesick for the members of her close, extended family. "These feelings hit me hard, and left me so guilty and so unprepared for my son, Rob's, state of simmering resentment. He was furious about being torn from his cousins and his beloved grandparents."

Of course, for Abbie, there had been real gain involved in undergoing these changes—the happily unfolding relationship with Owen—but for Rob, the new marriage had been yet more change after the cascade of changes initiated by the initial divorce. It involved fresh losses too: not only the upheaval and the move, far from anyone he knew, but also the loss of his single parent's exclusive attention. Abbie was in love and distracted, and her son couldn't help feeling she'd forsaken him for this new person in her life.

It is this basic state of affairs, which emerges ineluctably in a large number of remarriage situations, that creates the architectural model of remarriage. The central theme of this model is that the new marriage sets into motion the development of a family structure involving individuals who are stuck insiders and those who are stuck outside the existing emotional system. This makes a second or later marriage very different from a nuclear, first-family type of organization.

In this marriage, Abbie Jamison was the ultimate insider, carrying on an exhausting, unending shuttle diplomacy between her new romantic partner and her beloved son, with whom she'd shared a long, exclusive, single-parent history. Owen Jamison was the newcomer/outsider, shocked to find himself being shunned by his stepson and having difficulty gaining entry into the preexisting group's shared culture—their set of understandings about the trivial happenings of daily life (for example, what is an insolent comment, and what a playful tease?). This fixed insider/outsider structure, so emblematic of the architectural model, is one that most remarrying couples, heady with amorous plans for a better and happier future, rarely anticipate.

"The difficulties about being a stepfather were unexpected and very painful for me," Owen recounted. "It took a lot of getting used to, and finally, I went to a therapist who suggested that maybe I shouldn't even expect Rob to like me—that what was happening was a normal thing, and I should start to come to terms with it—which I did. But then there came a time when Rob started indicating that I wasn't so bad, after all. We're pretty close now."

"How long did that take?" I asked, pleasantly surprised to hear the news.

Owen steepled his fingers, looked down at them thoughtfully. "I think it was about three years."

Two splashes of high color had appeared in Abbie's cheeks. "Rob was in junior high then. He just started coming around, and one day he asked if he could have a private conversation with Owen in the living room. They closed the door."

"Tell me about that," I said.

Abbie turned to her husband, touched his knee. "You tell her. I wasn't in the room, but I was dying of curiosity."

"We had a good, long heart-to-heart, but the upshot of it was that Rob said he realized that he had been rejecting me since the marriage, and he apologized." Owen's face was suffused with pleasure as he recalled that experience. "We're pretty close now," he repeated.

It had taken time—three difficult years—but from that time onward, the basic structure of the family had undergone a slow but steady renovation process, and Owen was now a welcome and comfortable insider.

DISCIPLINE

As we know, families create an invisible boundary around themselves so that all the members know who the people on the inside are and who exists in the world outside the intimate group. However, divorced and remarried families must create "a boundary with a hole in it" to facilitate the children's easy access to and from the domicile of the ex spouse who is the other parent. In the Jamisons' case, one might have said their family boundary had two holes because the offspring of two prior marriages existed. However, Owen's sons were out of touch with their mother, and no traffic between his former wife and his newly formed family existed.

I asked Abbie about Rob's relationship with his dad, and her expression seemed to tighten. "What about it?" she asked me warily, her lips forming a straight, thin line.

"Are they close?"

The question elicited a sigh. "No, Rob has a lot to forgive his father for. A lot. Although I do, too. We both bore the brunt of Gary's anger as I was getting out of the marriage. Also, Gary would try to get at me by doing things that were harmful to our son."

"What sorts of things?" I asked.

"Oh, he traveled a great deal and he would take this little kid with him on vacations to Central America. Once there, he would start dating a woman who didn't even speak English and whom Rob had never met, and she would travel with them. This would happen when Rob was so little. And then the next time my son and his dad went on vacation together, there would be a different woman in the previous woman's place. Also, Gary was working much of the time; he was on his cell phone constantly. So this five-year-old kid was in this strange country where he didn't know the language, with a strange woman along, and his father was not really giving him much attention." Abbie's voice was taut with anger.

"That sounds pretty scary for a young child," I said sympathetically.

"Yes. So, luckily, I think my son has learned a different way to be a male from Owen." She shot a grateful glance at her husband. "Owen has been a kind and loving male model for Rob, something that Rob never had in his own father. Owen's been patient, steady, informed, consistent and just . . . *there* for him," she said. A moment later, though, she sighed and added, "Still, there was a period of time when Rob wasn't having any part of him. It was tense, really *hard*."

I turned to Owen. "In what ways was he being hard on you? By not speaking to you or by being insolent—or what?"

Owen's answer was directed to Abbie. "It was more often his insolence to you. I couldn't stomach it." He turned to me, "The way we handled it was that I didn't give him direct orders or tell him what to do. Most of the fresh talk and back talk was directed at Abbie, and that bothered me a lot."

"Generally speaking, how do you guys manage discipline?" I asked, and Abbie said that they would typically talk things over first, but she would be the one to manage the handing out of punishments and consequences.

I nodded approvingly, for the remarriage research findings do clearly indicate that the biological parent should always be the one in charge of meting out disciplinary actions. Abbie added, "Actually, there were a couple of times when Rob would behave very offensively with me, and Owen would step in. But that was rare, and he did it very gently," she assured me, while turning to bestow a brief fond glance on her husband.

SOFT-HARD-SOFT

Toward the end of this interview, I asked the Jamisons the following stock question: "The major problem in this relationship is . . . what?" Owen's cell phone rang at that moment, and after a brief glance at the name that came into view, he stepped into the front hallway to answer it.

Abbie and I waited. She was frowning, and three straight railroad tracks ran across her forehead.

"I think we have different temperamental styles," she said, as Owen returned to sit beside her on their dark velvet sofa. She turned to him as if responding to his question, not mine. "So I have learned to temper my passion, my—whatever you call it—my outspokenness."

"Do you mean your intensity?" I asked.

She turned back to me. "My intensity, yes. Although Owen is really, in a way, drawn to it, the force of my feelings can push him away if I'm not careful. I do have to be very solicitous, very tenderhearted, because he is so averse to conflict. I, on the other hand, feel that if there's something going on, it's best to get your cards on the table, and that can happen with a wham! The upshot has been that I've had to pay a great deal of attention to the ways in which I bring things up and the ways in which we discuss them. Because if I'm hopping mad and start yelling about some issue, I know that really is harmful to him. As a result, I've become able to modulate my strong feelings a lot and also present them to him very carefully."

I was impressed. Abbie Jamison, in her thoughtful, introspective way, seemed to have stumbled across the concept of soft-hard-soft, which, as noted above, is among the score of helpful coping strategies Papernow teaches her clients. As will be recalled, soft-hard-soft is a simple but remarkably helpful communication skill: it involves sandwiching a difficult message between two friendly, understanding expressions—one preceding and one following the problematic, difficult filling.

For example, Owen Jamison, worn down and deeply hurt by his stepson's coldly negative feedback, could have distanced himself from Rob and begun holding Abbie at fault for being too lax with her "impossible" offspring. As a result, Abbie might have become angrily defensive and critical of her "harshly demanding" spouse. The upshot would have been that the members of the pair became polarized and then withdrew to opposite corners of the marital fighting ring.

However, if Abbie were to forestall that by approaching Owen and first acknowledging his benign intentions and her concern—"I know that Rob's behavior is really tough on you, and I care about that a lot"—the interchange would start off on an understanding, sympathetic, calm note.

Then this soft statement could be followed by the sterner, more difficult message: "I know your patience is wearing thin, and you're finding it harder and harder to be friendly to him or even acknowledge his presence. You seem to bristle when he comes into a room. But can you grit your teeth and try to show him more compassion and friendliness?"

The hard part of the communication could then be mitigated by another soft message, one that might point a way toward an improved future. Abbie's soft closing remarks might be along the conciliatory, understanding lines of, "I know you think I need to be firmer with Rob, and it's true that knowing the hard time the kid has been through has made me cut him a lot of slack. But it's awful when he comes into a room and doesn't say hello to you and acts as if you aren't there. So I'm going to tell him he has to meet your eye, and he has to say hello to you at the same time he says hello to me. It would be great if you could greet him with some warmth when he does that. I do get it. I know how hard this is on you."

This soft-hard-soft kind of dialogue sets off a very different interpersonal exchange from the one in which Owen eventually snaps and begins snarling at Rob, calling him a rude, nasty brat, and Abbie leaps to her son's defense, calling her spouse (on extended trial as a father) a hard-hearted, browbeating bully of a man. An exchange of this kind could easily trigger a runaway quarrel—one in which no possible conclusion could ever be reached and both members of the fighting couple would soon stop hearing what the other one is saying.

Clearly the Jamisons were capable of preventing that from happening, and were also, as Owen told me, capable of backing up and starting over whenever a shouting match threatened. And although Abbie Jamison was a "temperamentally intense" person—someone who felt compelled to lay her cards on the table—she had managed to teach herself the necessary soft-hard-soft skills in order to lay those cards down very gently.

CHAPTER FIVE

Patterns of the Past: Greg and Caroline Meyer, 2011

The term "psychic bruises in bad places," used in the architectural model, actually encompasses a wealth of marital and family therapy theories about the ways in which the power of the past is experienced in our present day lives.

As Lily Pincus and Christopher Dare observe, we all have a tendency to get into repetitive patterns of relationships that harken back to what we have seen and known from our earliest days onward. "Sometimes, in marriage, the repetitive aspect of sequences of partnership is remarkably literal, as when a woman whose childhood was damaged by her father's alcoholism finds herself marrying a man who turns out to be an alcoholic, divorces him and then gets into the same situation once more," these famed clinicians write.

In short, people don't always learn from experience. Or they may learn the wrong thing from a negative experience and bounce themselves into the very opposite situation. For example, I interviewed a remarried couple in which the wife, the daughter of an incorrigibly faithless but beloved father, had left an exciting but sexually unfaithful first husband—someone much like her dad—and then married a stodgy, unemotional but reliable middle-management executive. She was bored, lonely, and unhappy.

The critical point is that we bring to our adult relationships internal models of being in a relationship we have known from earliest infancy onward. They may not be as blatantly obvious as Pincus and Dare's "alcoholic" example, but they do exist as our personal road maps—you could call them our internalized global positioning systems. Because they are the first truths of our existence, our family's patterns of being in intimate relationships are what we know: they are reality itself. Perhaps that is why, for so many individuals, the "way it was" seems like "the way it has to be."

Family therapist Patricia Meyer makes the same point in *The Family Life Cycle*. She states that a majority of people's "life course is grounded in a likeness or opposition to that of the parents. In other words an individual follows the behavioral patterns that he has experienced, or [he generates] behavioral patterns *opposite* to those experienced in growing up." Regardless of the direction he is moving in, he is using the same map as his reference point. We shall see how this played out in the several marriages of Greg Meyer.

CAROLINE'S STORY

Dr. Gregory Meyer, a tall, well-built seventy-one-year-old with springy blond graying hair and aquiline features, was the scion of a well-to-do German Jewish family. He had been raised in New York City and well educated in privileged schools, and he eventually studied medicine at Harvard Medical School. He now owned and ran a successful pediatric practice in Manhattan.

This solid, accomplished record was the bright side of Greg Meyer's story, but for many years, his personal life had taken on a darker tone. He had been through two unsuccessful marriages, both of which he viewed as "disasters" involving years of misery and self-recrimination. At the time of our interviews he was married to his third wife, Caroline Meyer, age sixty-eight. I asked them how long they had been together, and a Cheshire-cat smile came to both their faces. They looked at one another swiftly; then Caroline said, "It's about twenty-five years now."

I was seated opposite them in the comfortable living room of their large, sunny West Side apartment. I had my notepad on my lap and was jotting down comments as the conversation unfolded. I asked Caroline if she was employed, and she said that she was and had been for many years. Currently, she was a teacher at a private high school in the city. "How would you describe your first marriage?" I then asked her. "Or," I said hastily, "were you never married before?"

"Oh, I was," she said. She added nothing further.

"For how long?" I asked, my pencil poised over my notebook.

"Twenty-one years."

I looked up, surprised. "Whoa, that's a long marriage!" I said.

"Yes," she responded drily. "I hung in there."

I asked her the name of her ex-spouse; it was William. He had never remarried, lived in Vermont, and was totally out of her life, Caroline said, adding that her maiden name was Blum.

I asked her if she shared children with her ex-husband, and she replied almost curtly, "Two children—a son of thirty-nine and a son of thirty-six." Their father was out of their lives, she added quickly. "My boys have actually disassociated themselves from him completely." Her voice was flat.

She told me that her sons' names were John and Luke.

"That was her New Testament phase," said Greg. "She married out." He hesitated for a beat. "I did too." Caroline laughed. She had a friendly, open face, wide green eyes and bouncy, wavy gray hair.

Were there grandchildren? I asked. She nodded; her older son was married and had two children. His family lived in Weston,

Connecticut, within easy driving distance. She and Greg were close to them. Then she explained that the reason her married son was adamant about not having his "real," biological father coming around was that he didn't want his kids to have any contact with him.

For a moment I paused, tempted to go down that road, but I was worried lest Greg feel left out at this early phase of the interview. So I turned to him and told him it was his turn to answer the question. "Your first marriage—how would you describe it?"

"As something that happened long ago," he parried with a smile. Caroline laughed her easy laugh again.

"Oh no, I didn't hold back!" she protested against his nonresponse.

"You didn't really describe your marriage," replied Greg. "Why don't you go ahead?"

Caroline fell silent. At last she said, "The marriage was complicated. It was very complicated. I was so taken—so head-over-heels in love with this man who was six years older than me and living in Greenwich Village. It was all very romantic, and I felt as if a great new world was opening before me. His parents were blue-collar Irish, and he was a sort of hippie." She shrugged her shoulders.

"Were you yourself a hippie then?" I asked, gazing at her maroon, boat-necked sweater and the three silver chains around her neck.

She shook her head. "No, no, I was a student at Smith College. It was between my junior and my senior years, and I thought this Village life was wildly romantic. It was really hard on my parents, my middle-class parents, who had married poor and then built themselves up. I couldn't understand why they would object. Yes, Bill was penniless; but why couldn't he and I do the same thing they'd done?"

I smiled. "So you were downwardly mobile?"

"Yes, but I thought it was a great thing. At the time, my ex-husband was breaking away from his Midwestern background.

He was a dropout—a high school dropout—but eventually he got his degree. Ultimately he went to drama school. . . ." Her voice trailed off.

"What is he doing now? Is he earning a living?" I asked.

Caroline bit her lip. "No. For a while he was. He had actually gone on to get a degree in social work, and he was working as a child therapist at New York—Presbyterian Hospital. I believe he was very well thought of there until—well, he had a bad break-down and blew it all. It was really horrendous; he was so mean and so angry. Bill came from a very dysfunctional family with a lot of violence."

"Abuse," I said tentatively, and she nodded. "Did his father beat him?" I asked.

"Yes," said Caroline. "His father knocked the kids around a lot. Bill was the oldest, and he took the brunt of it. Finally, there came a point when he stood up to his dad and punched him out. Around the time that I met and fell in love with him, he was trying to remake himself, and he was pretty much succeeding. But things caught up with him. They caught up with him really badly."

Her facial expression was tense.

"Was he actually hospitalized?" I ventured.

"Yes," she said. "Yes. And as he approached that time—after-ward too, when he came home—he had some pretty obnoxious ways. He was particularly hard on our oldest son—not physically so much, but he was just so contemptuous, so rudely dismissive of him. It was an ongoing conflict."

I paused, thinking about how readily an abusive family pattern falls into the groove that, once created, continues to repeat itself. Here were an individual who had been abused as a child and an eldest son who had become caught up in a similar, unremitting battle. And, alas, it is well known that verbal abuse can have even more damaging consequences for children than outright physical attacks.

Glancing down at the notebook on my lap, I stared at the number of years that Caroline's first marriage had lasted. "Wow, twenty-one years of that," I said. "You were married to someone who became mean and hurtful and went crazy." I hesitated. "Could you describe your first marriage as crazy?" I asked her, my voice tentative.

"Well, yes," she said, "but it was mixed. There were good periods at first. It was the last seven or eight years that got really tough. It was just hard." It was fear that had made her hold on to the marriage, she said. "I didn't want to be an angry, embittered person. When my first husband was hospitalized after a suicide attempt, I had a fantasy that things would be better when he returned home. I thought it would all be hunky-dory, but it was awful. He was never what you could call a happy, supportive person, but he became so *nasty*—nastier than he had ever been before. He would make snide, obnoxious comments and attack me on any pretext—not physically but verbally, even though I'd supported him when he was getting his degrees."

"And he never forgave you for it," I said with a smile.

She laughed. "No good deed goes unpunished." She paused for a moment, then added, "Bottom line, it was a bad dynamic. And when our younger son Luke had a manic break—he's bipolar—the hospital recommended he not have any contact with his dad. They recommended the same for me. They didn't want to do family therapy; they wanted Bill out of the family picture completely."

Greg broke in at that moment to say, "He was a very, very scary guy. He has these thick arms, all big muscles. . . ."

"He's very scary," agreed Caroline, adding quickly, as if in Bill's defense, "but he's also very charismatic. He could be very charismatic—but he could be scary," she conceded.

I asked Greg if he had ever met Caroline's ex-husband, and he rolled his eyes. "The first weekend Caroline and I spent away, we went to Vermont. He called us up and said he was in Woodstock, the town we were in, and that he had a chainsaw and a hacksaw and he was going to come over and maim us as we had maimed him."

Caroline interjected that Bill had had numerous affairs and had even been pushing for an open marriage—a notion she had found unthinkable.

"The local police came," resumed Greg, "and it turned out Bill wasn't in Vermont at all. He was in New York City the whole time and was just trying to scare us."

I smiled. "Just making sure you had a fun weekend." The three of us laughed, and Caroline asked me if I wanted a refill of coffee. I shook my head, and we continued.

A TIME OF DESPERATE LONELINESS

When asked to describe the first of his two prior marriages, Greg cleared his throat and said, "Well, okay, my first marriage could be described as— a uh a mistake."

Caroline giggled. Greg's response was ridiculous on the face of it.

"What kind of a mistake?" I asked, as if his response had been a serious one.

"We had no real connection with one another, a fact that she was quicker to perceive than I was. When we met, I was in my third year of medical school. My parents were in the process of divorcing after twenty-seven years of an excruciating, terrible marriage. My younger sister was in a psychiatric hospital; she was suffering from schizophrenia and had been for several years. It was an illness that was to culminate in her suicide."

He stopped. I stared at him. "Awful," I said feelingly. I paused, thinking that this successful physician had grown up as the small, dependent witness to a harrowing example of what being in an intimate relationship is like.

I asked him how old he had been when his sister died.

"Twenty-three," he said. I scribbled a few lines on my notepad. One was the record of his age at the time of his sister's death, and the other was the observation that mental illness had been a potent issue in both Greg and Caroline's lives.

"I'm giving you this background because I was hit hard by all of these things and at sea in a way I scarcely comprehended while it was happening," Greg went on. "I felt so alone with it, desperately lonely. I was in my third year of medical school, hating it and feeling out of place there. I was just lost. Then I met this very striking Dutch woman who had come over on a year's exchange to work in a laboratory. Her name was Gaby Mertens, and I somehow persuaded myself that I was smitten by this very beguiling Netherlander who spoke only moderately good English, but in a very charming way. She was my life raft, and I talked her into getting married to me—which we did after knowing each other only three months."

His tone of voice had become sarcastic, a dig directed against his earlier self.

I asked how long the marriage had lasted. Nine years, he replied. They had become the parents of a daughter, now forty-seven, and a son, forty-five. "Their names are Sallie and Daniel. Sallie had a very atypical development. She has what is now known as Asperger's syndrome, which is a less severe form of autism. Fortunately, she's had a fairly benign course and now has a significant other and a good job mapping natural resources with a computer company. Apparently she's remarkably good at it," Greg said proudly.

His son Dan had emigrated to Denmark and married a Danish woman, an anthropologist. He'd lived there ever since, supporting himself by teaching English and translating.

Caroline smiled and said, "Dan and his wife are both a little nuts, but they are adorable, and we have a wonderful time when we see them. We're going over there in a few days."

"But I'm not sure they should ever have kids," commented Greg, suggesting to me that the pair had a somewhat giddy, eccentric quality about them.

"So then how would you describe that first marriage?" I asked once again. "Nine years is a long time."

"It was a mistake," he repeated

I smiled. "What went on during the nine years of that mistake?"

He seemed at a loss. Finally he said, "Very little. It petered out. But I didn't realize how bad things had gotten, because I have a vulnerability to aloneness and I end up clinging to things. The more dicey things get, the more I cling, and the more blind I get to reality."

"You're saying she was on her way out?"

"She was on her way out, and she finally made it clear to me. It took me two years to actually get the point, but I finally did. So I left. Looking back, I would describe that marriage as very distant, cold, disconnected," said Greg, looking dispirited. I thought of the relational model presented to him as a young boy and made a mental memorandum to inquire more about his parents' marriage.

"But from what you told me, you were busy doing your own thing, too," Caroline reminded him, as if wanting to bring him back from the dark place to which he'd gone.

"I've always been busy doing my own thing," he responded. He had completed his internship and been in the service during this time, stated his wife. "That's true," said Greg, "and I did my residency."

"Raised the children," prompted Caroline.

"Yes, the residency," Greg's voice was rueful. "Raised them by not being around."

I asked him if his ex-wife was still close to the children, and he said that she was, more or less. "For many years she bad-mouthed me to them and turned them away from me. It wasn't until a few years ago—around five years or so—that my son Dan was visiting Gaby's cousins in Holland, and these cousins told him he had it all backward. They said, 'Your father is a good guy, and your mother is really destructive.' Actually, Gaby had been doing some pretty crazy stuff all along."

"Crazy in what way?" I asked.

Greg's lips tightened. "All sorts of things. She took up with a hippie some while after our divorce, and that was disastrous as far as the kids were concerned."

I was distracted momentarily as I wrote down this information. The hippie, that romantic free spirit so celebrated in the 1960s— who lived in the moment and defied social conventions—had appeared in both of the Meyers' life narratives.

"So, on the second marriage," Greg prompted me, as if to shake me from my reverie.

"Don't say 'It was a mistake'!" I teased him.

He shook his head, said no danger; "I would describe it as the most unmitigated disaster in the history of the northeastern United States." He was smiling, making fun of his own exaggeration, and yet I could see that he meant it.

MARITAL HATRED

Greg Meyer's second wife was named Celia, and when I asked him to tell me something about what that marriage had been like, he wasn't at all evasive. "It was hideous. It was disgusting. Celia was sadistic. I was masochistic. She wanted me to disown my kids from my first marriage, said they weren't my children anymore."

I frowned. "That must have been incredibly hard on you." Greg nodded, looking upset, but said nothing. "Did you and Celia have children together?" I asked.

Greg said they had had a son, now thirty-five, and a daughter, age thirty-three.

I added their names to my growing list—Nathaniel and

Margo—then looked up into Greg's troubled face. "So these two kids grew up in that 'hideous, sadomasochistic' atmosphere?" I asked.

It was Caroline who responded. "They did, for a certain amount of time—"

"—Until my second wife died of breast cancer when they were nine and seven years old, so the marriage lasted for twelve years, all told," Greg explained. "Celia was a glacial WASP beauty," he went on. "She had a kind of cool, aristocratic air, like Ingrid Bergman or Grace Kelly. I was amazed. I could not believe that an ordinary Jewish boy like me would be desired by such a goddess."

Caroline laughed nervously. I said drily, "You got lucky."

"Yes. Well, this goddess turned out to be extraordinarily stupid, narrow-minded, and spiteful," said Greg, a barely suppressed anger in his voice. "Extraordinarily possessive," he continued. "And part of the reason she didn't want these children who were, quote, 'not my children anymore,' was that she didn't want them to have any of the family's resources. For Celia, money was the great metaphor—money was love."

Had she really tried to stop him from paying basic child support for the children of his first marriage? I asked, for I found this hard to believe. I knew that some remarried wives resented deeply these payments to former mates, but Celia's position seemed so extreme. Greg said that she *had,* vociferously, and she'd even concocted a scheme to have the children come live with them for awhile in order to stop the outflow of child-support payments. "That didn't last long," Greg said with an ironic laugh.

"She wasn't nice to them," said Caroline quietly.

"It was awful," said Greg. "I'm still very critical of myself for not having found the gumption or having the smarts to know how to deal firmly with her manipulations."

I wondered whether Greg, having been the frightened, passive witness of his parents' traumatic marriage, had found himself without the voice or the resolve to stand up for the children of his former marriage in the face of the rageful Celia's resistance. She had behaved as if his love for his children were a betrayal of their own relationship.

"It sounds as if you were the one-down partner, the wounded bird, in both those marriages." My voice was cautious.

"Yes, I feel like I should have known better." Greg sounded remorseful. "I should have known better," he repeated. "I should have known what I know now." He turned to Caroline and took her hand in his. "I should have been married to a better, nicer woman." He looked at her lovingly. "As I am now."

MY LIFE CAN BEGIN NOW

Looking down at my hastily scribbled notes, I was reminded of the previous generation of Greg's family—specifically of the "excruciating, terrible" relationship that had ended in divorce after twenty-seven years. "Would you say your parents were in a sadomasochistic marriage?" I asked him.

Not unexpectedly, he said that they had been. "It was awful, just horrible. Basically, they were detached from one another, and my mother was pretty crazy, always very close to the edge. She would fly into these fantastic rages," Greg recounted.

I asked him if either of his earlier wives had flown into similar kinds of rages, and he said that his first wife had simply been emotionally disengaged. His second wife, on the other hand, *had* flown into rages—but she had done so in a different way. "With my mother, there were periods of calm, and then these sorts of psychotic storms. With Celia, it was a steady stream of hatefulness."

Greg leaned toward me intently, folding both hands between his knees. "I'm going to make a complicated statement—something that represents an inner state of mind that's far more mixed and complex than this may sound to you. But Celia's getting breast cancer and dying of it after three years was one of the happier events of my life, because it freed me of a pain that was just unendurable."

I said nothing, but felt my cheeks reddening. This was in fact one of the forbidden, embarrassing thoughts I myself had been thinking.

"I remember the day that she died." Greg's voice was low and musing. "A weight just completely lifted off me, and I thought, 'My life can begin now.' Celia had somehow convinced me—and a whole circle of people around us—that I was the biggest son of a bitch, the nastiest, most terrible person imaginable. She went out of her way to tell everybody how dreadful I was. She did a real number on me, and that, plus my less-than-marvelous self-esteem, managed to convince me that I was one of the worst, most awful people around."

He sighed, almost a groan. Then he looked at his wife, said in a more comfortable voice, "I bounced back, though. Caroline and I found each other. She mothered my younger children in the most extraordinary way, and they've turned out to be terrific people, particularly my daughter Margo," he said, looking well pleased.

This daughter had become a physician, like her dad. She was now married to a physician, and the pair had one child. I gazed at Greg, struck by the triumphal tone in his voice as he'd reported his reaction to his second wife's death: *My life can begin now!* It was as if he had paid off a kind of debt to the last generation, one that had prevented his life from beginning much earlier in his adulthood.

Both of his earlier marriages had been, when one thought about it, iterations of the patterns of the past. In the first instance, his hasty marriage to his Dutch wife, the relationship had been characterized by the disconnectedness and emotional distance with which he had been familiar from boyhood onward. That marriage had been a faithful reenactment of what he knew about men, women, and intimate relationships.

In his second marriage, there had been an emotional connection, though the emotions involved were those of anger, contempt, and hatred. Greg's past, in his family of origin, had also invaded his present in the form of his second wife's "craziness," periodic tirades, and accusatory outbursts. In both these "disastrous" relationships, his family's global positioning system had been the knowledge base from which he'd operated; it had provided the map and the driving directions. The statement that his life could begin now meant, it seemed to me, that at last he was free to move off the (unconsciously) designated pathway and make a major course correction. His first marriage had been cold and emotionally disengaged, and his second marriage had been hot with anger and vindictiveness. In this marriage to Caroline, he had finally gotten it right.

WE WOULD JUST CLING TO EACH OTHER

I asked the partners about what fantasies they'd had about remarrying. How did they think the new marriage would differ from their prior marriages? What parts of those premarital fantasies had come true, and what parts were very different from what they'd imagined?

This topic seemed to stump them, and neither answered for a period of time. Finally, Caroline said, "It's interesting, but I can't remember what the fantasies were. I know I assumed that things were going to get a heck of a lot better, because they couldn't get much worse." She laughed, and I wasn't sure why. Then she said, "No, just that I was teaming up with a really reasonable person who had a delightful sense of humor—"

"Nobody's ever said that to me before," Greg interrupted her coyly.

She laughed and bumped her shoulder against his. "Oh, that is not true. That's so not true." Then, in a more serious tone of voice,

she addressed me. "Truly, it's quite delightful. If anything bothers me about Greg—any little thing, and there are a few of them
that do—he's so introspective and will hear me out and think
over what I've said. My theory is that we both spent many years
cowering—living with partners who were hateful, sadistic people—and this marriage has given us a chance to flex our muscles
with each other, and speaking our minds is just not a problem."

"Feels wonderful," said Greg, to which Caroline added that
there was a lot more give-and-take in this relationship. "So we're
really lucky," she concluded happily. After a brief silence, though,
she frowned and said, "What was difficult was having the four
kids in the house at once."

Greg then explained that they'd not only had Caroline's two
children and his two motherless children, but that his nonres-
ident older children also visited them frequently. He shook his
head back and forth as if to say it had been mind-boggling:
"There was just so much *stuff* to deal with that we worked out a
theory that whatever trouble a kid got up to could be blamed on
the absent partner. Because Caroline's ex was out of the picture,
living somewhere in Vermont, and of course, mine was dead—"

"So if we saw any bad behavior in one of the kids, we could
always say, 'It's his fault,' or, 'It's her fault,'" Caroline chimed in
merrily.

"Did that prove helpful?" I asked them, and Greg said that
they'd joked about it a lot, but it was not easy having all these
kids from different households. "Just dealing with their issues
about getting along with each other—it was a challenge." He
halted there, the color rising in his cheeks. I nodded, thinking of
the fact that they had needed to work out a common ground that
would unite three differing family cultures.

"A challenge." I repeated Greg's word aloud. "What kinds of
issues with each other did these three sets of children have?"

"It was Greg's oldest child from his second marriage mostly,"
said Caroline. "Nathaniel and his father had bonded with great

intensity during the years of his mother's illness. They played hockey and other sports, and Greg took Nat everywhere. So when Celia died and Greg got involved with me, Nathaniel didn't lose only his mother; he felt he lost his father, too. He lost both parents, basically. Plus, he'd been the oldest kid in his first home, and in our home there were my two older boys, who could squelch this kid." She laughed. "They actually used to sit on him sometimes, because he could be very argumentative and in your face, and very, very difficult."

Greg laughed, too. "I remember coming home and finding Nat yelling and Caroline's son Luke sitting on him, peacefully reading a book!" He shrugged his shoulders and held out his hands in a gesture of helplessness. "So it was—yes—an awful lot to deal with." I laughed with them, but what flashed into my mind was Dr. Lucile Duberman's clinical observation on birth order and remarriage. "In the case of the reconstituted family," Duberman writes, "there are two 'first-born' children, which doubles the likelihood of and intensity of disorder."

Nathaniel had lost his familiar "oldest child in the household" status when his dad brought him to live in Caroline's house with two older stepbrothers. Adding to the boy's difficulties were his father's two even older children by his first marriage, who came to stay on a regular basis. Earlier on he had been the treasured oldest son in his dad's second marriage, as well as Greg's close companion during Celia's three-year illness. Now Nathaniel was lost somewhere in the middle of the new family, and he'd shown his displeasure by becoming disruptive and combative.

"As for Margo, Nathaniel's younger sister," said Caroline from out of nowhere, "she and I bonded very slowly and naturally—and it was lovely. That was all right with my boys, but I knew the disparity between Greg and their real, biological dad, who was basically a fuck-up, was something that was on my children's minds. Their father had thrown his career away and had so many problems, and had made a suicide attempt and been hospitalized.

Then here's Greg, who went to Brown and Harvard and has a medical practice, and whose kids are functioning okay. Actually, all four kids went to the same school, so that was something that they had in common. They did grow up together, in this very apartment." She looked toward the doorway as if expecting one of them to come in and join us.

"Are you saying that your kids were aware that they had a defective father and that you had brought in this effective father—and wasn't that good for them?" I asked her. I did realize that her children might have had a terrible loyalty bind: the more they identified with Greg, the more they would lose whatever internalized shreds remained of their true, biological dad.

She nodded. "It was. It was very good for them in lots of ways." Her voice sounded uncertain. She turned to Greg. "But they all made relationships with you in different ways," she said to him. "And are still making them, but they are not the same kinds of bonds. It couldn't happen; they were already teenagers." There was an undertone of disappointment in her voice.

Greg looked somewhat discomfited. He cleared his throat, then said, "Caroline's relationships with my children, especially Margo, have been a great source of strength for them. But I have not—maybe I am not—capable of forming that kind of closeness with my stepkids, and I haven't pushed myself on them. I don't think they have sought me out in any particularly close way, so I've been a tolerant and affectionate but more distant stepparent."

Despite his seeming self-blame on this score, I believed it was actually wise for Greg to keep his distance and allow his stepchildren the time and space in which to get to know him. And it was clear that Caroline's abundant warmth and goodwill flowed out to fill any vacuum that might otherwise have appeared in these relationships.

"Adolescence—that's a particularly tough time," I said with an appreciative nod.

Caroline sighed. "A very tough time, so it was hard. It was

really hard. We had our share of issues to work through—disciplinary issues, and oh my gosh, we would just *cling* to each other."

"We did," said Greg fervently. "We still do."

Caroline breathed a deep sigh. "These days we're on our own and happy to say that the kids are all doing pretty well—a couple of them spectacularly well. And we all get together for Thanksgiving—all six children and their families. Even Greg's first wife, Gaby, comes for Thanksgiving dinner, as does his half-brother, Jack. He's the son of the woman Greg's dad married later on, after the divorce," she explained.

I turned to Greg, surprised. "Your first wife joins you for Thanksgiving?"

"Yup," he said, a mischievous smile spreading across his face. "We spend one day a year pretending that all the old animosities have been resolved."

CHAPTER SIX

Boundless Trust: Carole and Ted Burke, 1997 and 2010

THE BURKES IN 1997

During my first round of remarriage research in 1997, I was a reg-ular attendee at one of the nationwide stepfamily support groups that brought together remarried couples as a way of facilitating discussions of the common issues they were facing. Not only did I play the role of the fly on the wall at these sessions; I also con-ducted separate interviews with many of the re-wed partners who attended, meeting them either in their houses or at my home office.

It was at one of these meetings that I met Carole and Ted Burke, who had then been married for three and a half months. It became evident to me shortly after she'd begun speaking that Carole had entered her remarriage secure in the happy fantasy that Ted's young-adult children would have little impact upon their newly consecrated relationship.

Carole Burke was a slim, well-turned-out businesswoman in her late thirties or thereabouts. Everything she wore had clearly been chosen with care: striped suit-blouse, gray tweed jacket, black skirt, gold and onyx earrings, low-heeled black pumps. Her husband, Ted, who looked about a decade older, was dressed more casually. He wore a soft T-shirt with a collar underneath a blue sweater and slightly rumpled chinos.

There were seven couples present (plus me), and we all sat in a circle. This evening's meeting had begun with an icebreaker: each person was to introduce himself or herself and describe something positive that had happened during the course of the previous week. When it came to the Burke couple's turn, I wasn't too surprised that it was Carole who spoke out first.

"I'm Carole Burke," she said briskly, then turned to look at her husband full-face and said wryly, "and this reluctant gentleman to my right is Ted."

All eyes turned to him. Ted was a solidly built man with brownish-blond hair, a broad brow, and a benign expression on his face. He sat back in his wooden chair in a posture of complete relaxation and acquiescence, his arms folded. Yet even before his wife's tart remark, I'd had the strong sense that a part of him wasn't really here.

Carole was just the opposite; very present, filled with determination and electricity. The major problem she was dealing with at this moment, she stated without further ado, was that she did not have children of her own but that Ted's two grown children lived with them. "I am finding it tremendously hard adjusting to living with three people," she said, then stopped herself short, recalling the task at hand. "Let's see, did anything good happen to us this week?" she asked uncertainly, turning to her spouse.

"It's *all* been positive," stated Ted.

She paused briefly, then nodded. "It's pretty much positive. It's not really bad, but . . . I'm just stressed out, I think." She fell silent, as did the rest of us. Ted's goodwill had silenced not only Carole but everyone else in the group.

At last someone asked her quietly if she wanted to add anything, perhaps tell us the children's ages. Carole nodded and said resentfully, "Katie is almost twenty-two, and Brian's twenty-four, and they're both still living with us."

Ted cleared his throat, then said in a tone of concession that it was true that the adjustments she was being forced to make were far greater than the adjustments he was making, and this was "because of the situation with the kids." But he added that as far as he was concerned, they really were still "the kids"—they always would be "the kids" no matter how old they were. "I take for granted the fact that they're there, they've always been there, I've always had them."

His voice took on an edge of reproof as he explained that he'd had sole custody of his children ever since their mother had walked out on the family when the children were teenagers. However, he did realize that it was a whole new world for Carole: "She continually reminds me that they're not kids, they're adults; but they will be *my* kids ad infinitum. And they are good kids. The fact is, when my wife—my first wife— deserted, my daughter took over the kitchen. Katie was just fourteen or fifteen, but she would say, 'Come on, we're going chopping,' and haul me to the grocery store. I'd never been to a grocery store in my life!" Ted's brief laugh was the laugh of a pleased parent, but his wife's expression tightened.

Ted went on to say that he was in law enforcement—he was a cop—and he'd seen a lot of the bad things that could happen when kids grew up in troubled family environments. "Knock on wood, neither one of my kids has ever gotten involved with drugs. They're at the point now where they'll go out and party and have a few drinks, but the serious kind of stuff doesn't happen. I've never had reason to believe that it *has* happened," he said assuredly, "but I know that Carole goes ballistic every time she opens the refrigerator and sees the way things are thrown around inside."

This addendum sounded like a change of subject, but Ted simply shrugged, his expression amiable as ever. He said that the only problem he was having was adjusting to his wife's adjusting. "It's a kind of double jeopardy," he said in a mildly amused tone.

His meaning was unclear to me. Was it that he was doing all the adjusting for both of them? Ted shot his wife an indulgent, paternal look and said that as far as he was concerned, it would be hard to pick out one good thing that had happened in this past month. It had all been pretty positive ever since they'd gotten married.

Do I Want to Be in This House?

Since Carole had no children of her own, it seemed to me that her transition from courtship to remarriage should have been an easy one. Ted's two children were young adults and presumably able to take care of themselves—aside from the obvious fact that they hadn't yet proved capable of moving out and living on their own. Yet compared to some of the other remarried couples in this group who were dealing with defiant, rebellious children and bitter, troublemaking ex-spouses, the Burkes appeared to be living in a relatively uncluttered situation.

Still, Carole was feeling alone and estranged in the unfamiliar world that was supposed to be her new home, and she stated that these feelings sometimes took on an almost unbearable intensity. "It isn't that we're having problems with the kids or anything like that," she conceded, her tone one of mollification. "And Ted and I *do* get along very well. But there's still a feeling that I have . . . our lifestyles have been very different."

She paused a moment, then said, "So a part of me is asking, 'Do I want to be in this house?' And another part of me is saying, 'Okay, my furniture is here, and my cat is here, so I guess I live here.'" For a moment she looked baffled, but then she turned, looked at Ted, and said with unexpected heat, "But I don't really live there. It's not mine!"

He flushed but didn't respond.

Clearly, as the latecomer in a firmly established family system, Carole was feeling as if she didn't belong. She was now positioned as the female head of the Burke household, but the rhythms of daily life that held sway there were none of her own making. It was Ted's family and his family's house. I wondered at that moment whether the painful outsider feelings she was now experiencing could perhaps have been expected and possibly prepared for in advance.

No sooner had that thought popped into my mind than Carole said flatly that well before her marriage, she had tried to do some troubleshooting about the kinds of problems that might arise. "I'm a very organized person, so I sat down with Ted's kids and explained to them that this was going to be a difficult transition for me, having been divorced and on my own for these past eleven years," she recounted, her gaze sliding around the circle and landing briefly on each person present.

"I told the kids that I loved their father and wanted to make this marriage work. 'But,' I said, 'he still thinks of you as children. I didn't know you as children—and you're twenty-two and twenty-four—so I think of you as adults—adults who are like roommates or housemates. And I've had housemates in the past, so there are a few things I want to make sure everybody understands.'"

Carole had then presented Ted's children with a few suggested "rules for living together." First of all, she'd assured them that what they did in their wing of the house was their own business, and she would respect their privacy scrupulously. But, she'd added, there were some areas in their home that were common areas, for example, the living room and the kitchen. "I explained to them that something that really bothers me are pots, pans, and dishes left sitting in the sink."

An irritable expression settled on her mobile, expressive face. "Now I can't actually understand why that should happen when there's a dishwasher right there," Carole said. "I mean, *Open the door.*

Put the dishes in. But these days, when I come home and find the dishes dripping all over the counters and the wastebaskets overflowing, I can't help but think, 'I'm now living with two roommates who don't contribute anything financially and don't do any helping out around the house either.' And this is my problem."

She folded her hands in her lap, sat up straight like an embarrassed but determined schoolgirl, looked around at the others with very wide, bright, staring eyes. "*My* problem is: Am I being unrealistic? Because this is driving me nuts." Then she reiterated in a voice tinged with exasperation and impotence that while the children might still be kids in her husband's eyes, she saw them as adults—adults whom the pair of them were supporting, although they themselves were dealing with some serious money issues at this time.

Carole wasn't actually crying, but her eyes were tearing up.

I Just End Up Feeling Crazy

Ted Burke sat with his arms folded across his chest wearing the almost professionally neutral expression of a policeman. He didn't appear disturbed in any way. It was as though he were equipped with some sort of a protective coating that shielded him from the torrent of distress raining down on him. He simply shrugged affably and said, "I guess I haven't been the disciplinarian that I might have been, but my kids never gave me any problems, so I really didn't see the need to—"

"Am I being unrealistic?" Carole cut in swiftly. "Ted says all of these things are minor things, and what's the big deal? That it's a problem only if you *think* it's a problem."

Without replying, Ted looked at his wife pointedly and held up an arm in a gesture of stopping traffic. To my surprise, it worked: she fell silent. Then he said in a low, measured voice that he was the custodial parent and had taken care of his children ever since his first wife left him and the marriage ended. "They look out for their end of the house," he said resolutely, adding that throughout these past seven years, Katie and Brian had taken over all of the cooking and managed most of the housework as well.

This sounded reasonable on the surface, but Carole heard it as blaming and upsetting. "The kids like to cook for themselves because they get in late, and that's *fine*," she burst in to say. "But when they're finished, the dishes end up on the counter or just sitting in the sink! I get to the point where I'm so *angry* that I want to break every single thing! I just throw it all in the dishwasher and mutter, 'Dammit, what is wrong here? Are these people so immature that they don't know how to pick up a dish? And then I get mad at myself, like— Ah, well, I just end up feeling crazy."

Her anger had boomeranged and landed on herself. She blinked her eyes several times in rapid succession. This home was Ted's and his children's domain. She felt like a somewhat problematic, barely tolerated visitor.

Blurred Boundaries

An important element factoring into this new marriage was Ted's long period of living alone with his children in a single-parent family structure. And as we know, what one typically sees in this kind of emotional system is the emergence of extremely intimate parent-child relationships. What had occurred almost reflexively in the wake of the mother's abandonment was that Ted's daughter, Katie, had moved in very close to her father in order to fill the vacuum in her abandoned parent's life.

In the process, she had inevitably gained extra power— the power that accompanies being needed and assuming extra responsibilities—and the boundary between the generations had become blurred. Katie Burke, at age fourteen, had taken on the role of female head of the household. She had been in charge of buying and cooking the family's dinner, so she would customarily make many of the normally "grown-up" choices—deciding, for example, what the family dinner would be in terms of what was bought and what eaten.

In a variety of ways, Katie had gained more authority relative to her remaining parent than she ever could have attained had there been no marital failure. So she and her older brother, Brian, had moved up a notch in the family hierarchy and were functioning as two semi-peers to their dad when this new person—this stranger, Carole—was suddenly introduced in a role that outranked their own positions in the family system. Carole's entry upon the scene was therefore bound to intrude on Ted's children's customary turf with her own needs for time, space, recognition, and authority.

Insiders and Outsiders

One of the primary challenges of remarriage had emerged in high relief in the course of this first encounter with the Burkes: that of the architecturally inbuilt stuck-insider and stuck-outsider positions that typically emerge in remarried family structures. Carole, the outsider, was frustrated by her failure to enter and influence her new family's ways of being; Ted, the insider member of the old, established system, was trying to keep the peace between the new woman in his life and the Burke family's time-worn, familiar ways of being.

Yet another allied challenge had to do with the confrontation between two divergent family cultures. As far as Ted's children were concerned, letting the pots and dishes sit in the sink had been perfectly acceptable behavior before their father's remarriage. Now the failure to rinse and put them away was being redefined (by his new wife, a foreign element) as a sign of "immaturity" and disrespect. And for her part, Carole, when she came home after work and saw those dishes sitting there, felt trampled upon and helpless.

As she blurted out sometime toward the close of that stepfamily meeting, the first and only one the Burkes attended, "I really do love Ted, and we're a good couple, but I also think about my *own* needs. And I don't want to live where I'm going to be uncomfortable, where I'm going to be afraid to say anything to his kids directly, where I'm walking around on eggshells!" She was feeling sidelined, alone, as if she were the first person on the planet to have ever experienced this welter of loving and angry and alienated feelings.

Such confusion is typical of early remarriage, when the newcomer to the family system is struggling to alter the system to suit her own rhythms and needs and is finding the emotional system resistant. She had expected that her new husband's household would shift about in ways that would make her feel more comfortable and at home. Hadn't she explained the situation to Ted's children in advance? But what she was discovering, with a shock of alarm (was this, her second marriage, to fail as had the first one?) was that the family had no interest whatsoever in changing.

Just the opposite: a phenomenon that remarriage experts Carolyn and Jack Bradt name, very simply, "Go Back!" was emerging. This phrase refers to the huge counterpressures that are generated when a foreign body (the stepparent) is introduced into an existing emotional system (the family). As the Bradts observe, a systemic change of this magnitude frequently produces a reactive surge in a backward direction—dedicated to getting rid of or at least neutralizing the effects of the intruder. This happens in a quasi-automatic fashion in much the same way that the body attempts to reject a transplanted organ that is perceived as "different" and "alien." In other words, the system swings into action in an effort to make things go back to the way they were before the new marriage came into existence.

Rephrased in the language of the architectural model, this is a description of remarriage challenge two—children's losses—and the overly close relationships that tend to develop among the surviving members of the family group.

Earlier Sorrows

When I interviewed the Burkes privately several weeks after the stepfamily group meeting, Carole told me that she felt she'd gotten a lot out of that session. She had felt validated by hearing from the other members of the group that her responses were completely normal and that she wasn't being "crazy" at all. However, Ted had been made uncomfortable by the level of personal revelation that emerged during the evening, and both of them felt that their own difficulties weren't nearly as serious as those of the other couples present. So they had decided not to go back again.

Nevertheless, when I met with the partners in their ranch-style home in Cheshire, Connecticut, I soon became aware that many of their issues were still simmering. On this occasion, both Carole and Ted (much to my surprise) were very willing to open up and participate in a self-revelatory discussion. I'd begun the conversation by telling them that in order to better understand where they were now as a couple, I'd have to know more about where each of them had come from.

I'd already learned that both of their previous marriages had ended in divorce. It was upon this landscape of former marital losses that the Burkes' new, more inclusive family civilization had to be established.

Carole told me that she had been married at age twenty-three to her first husband, Don, who was twenty-five at the time. That marriage, as she described it, had been "fun and separate," by which she meant that they'd gone their own ways a good deal of the time but had "had fun with our friends" when together. Throughout the five-year duration of the marriage, the pair had agreed that they would postpone having children. Unlike most of the people they knew, who were already starting families, they'd wanted to wait until they could afford to settle down and buy a home of their own. "At last, we did buy a house, after patiently saving for it during those years, but a month later my husband left. Just like that. It was December 7, 1986." Carole's voice had dropped an octave; she looked devastated.

"Pearl Harbor Day," I said reflexively.

"Yes," she said soberly, "that's the day he told me that he didn't want to be married anymore. He just woke up one morning and said that. I was taking business courses at the time, and I still remember the chapter; I remember the *page* I was reading when he told me. I will never forget that moment." Her nostrils flexed as she inhaled deeply.

I realized that the phrase *sneak attack* was running through my mind. Carole continued: "The way it happened was that he kept pacing back and forth, back and forth, and I asked him what was wrong. And he kept saying, 'I don't know how to tell you this, I don't know how to tell you this,' so I said, 'Just tell me what's wrong.' And all he said was, 'I don't want to be married anymore.'"

He'd had no reason for his behavior, no rationale to offer her. It wasn't until some eight years after their divorce that she'd gotten any kind of explanation from him. At that late date, her former spouse had apologized profusely and told her that he was honestly sorry about the way things had happened. He'd explained that he just hadn't felt at all ready to start having a family and hadn't known how to tell her. "Since now we had the house, he figured that it would be the time for us to have kids, and he'd realized that he just didn't want them."

Carole said that the sudden, inexplicable ending of her marriage had left her traumatized. "I never knew what I did wrong to cause the divorce, and it left me feeling so uncomfortable about dating, about being with other men. Because I was always thinking, 'What did I *do?*' and, 'Am I going to make the same mistakes?' And also, 'How do I need to change so the same kind of thing won't happen again?'"

Ted cleared his throat. "I had those same questions for a long time. I mean, how badly could I have acted? To this day I don't know what I did, but for a woman, a mother, to just walk out and leave her kids the way my first wife did—I don't get it! I don't have the answers, but I guess all the questions about it will remain in my mind forever." He slapped his hands on his thighs as though for emphasis.

Both Carole and Ted had come into this new relationship with histories that had left them feeling highly sensitized to the threat of further losses. Both of their former marriages had ended in an abrupt abandonment whose causes were mysterious.

In describing his own, much longer seventeen-year relationship, Ted said that his former marriage had been a very good and happy one until his ex-wife began drinking heavily. "We'd always been social drinkers, but there came a time when Liz was drinking more and more every day. I guess she couldn't sleep most nights, and she would get up at two a.m. and go out in the living room and sit and read a book, have a glass of brandy. Then she'd fall asleep in the chair and at noon or so wake up and start with the martinis. She'd be drinking those all day and into the evening." His voice was neutral, as if he were the reporter of rather than the participant in these disturbing events.

I asked him if he thought that his wife had been suffering from depression. Ted didn't miss a beat before shrugging, saying, "I haven't a clue." But then, as if to underscore his own lack of responsibility for his wife's emotional state, he began talking about the many sports activities and hobbies—golfing, boating, hiking—in which the whole family had been involved during that same period.

"Still, you're describing a deeply unhappy woman here," I said quietly.

Ted responded, "Apparently. But I didn't know it at the time."

Why hadn't he? I wondered. Whatever had been going on his first marriage, it seemed obvious that Ted had managed to keep his receiving dial turned to "off."

I glanced at Carole, who was clearly struggling so hard to be heard by him, to make him understand the sense of isolation she was experiencing as the stranger and outsider in his family's world. In the period of bewilderment and flux these partners were now experiencing, Ted needed to be able to develop his listening ears: the capacity truly to hear his partner out and register within himself her very real sense of internal pressure and disequilibrium. Carole, for her own part, needed to comprehend how poignantly attuned to his children's losses her new husband felt and how dedicated he was to defending them.

At present, though, each seemed cemented in his or her polar opposite stuck-insider or stuck-outsider position, unable to envision and empathize with the difficulties that the other person was experiencing.

A Zone of Privacy

Carole Burke had been in no way prepared for the fact that she and Ted were rarely alone and had almost no time to themselves. "That's been a real problem for me," she said, "because I'm aware of everything that's happening around me—when there's noise, when there are other people nearby. Ted is just oblivious to it, because as far as he's concerned, that's how it is: it's business as usual. Because it's always been like that for him."

Carole was referring to the obvious difference between first-time spouses and spouses in a later marriage, which is that the first-time-ever pair will generally experience a time of living alone and getting to know one another in a setting relatively free of intrusion. Couples like the Burkes, in a second marriage involving Ted's children, enter a different kind of situation, one in which the older, stronger sets of understandings are those shared by the biological parent and his offspring.

In a very real sense, this remarried family's new household was being constructed on land that still housed Ted's single-parent family's well-established, comfortable, settled ways of being. Given that she was a stranger to this up-and-running system's mutually understood norms and guides to action, it is easy to see why the neat and tidy Carole Burke was ready to assign moral interpretations ("lazy, inconsiderate") to such seemingly innocuous behaviors as whether the dishes were put into the dishwasher or left on the kitchen counter.

Attitudes about Money

As my conversations with the Burkes developed, it became ever clearer that their vastly differing views about money were another source of contention. At the time of their courtship, Ted had been in substantial financial difficulties. This was due to a long-term debt resulting from the failure of an auto parts business he'd formerly owned (it had gone belly-up during the recession of the 1980s). Carole had helped ameliorate this situation with a generous infusion of capital from her own life savings. She had lent Ted thirty thousand dollars during the period of their engagement.

Still, the couple's finances remained strained, and the partners soon discovered that they had serious differences when it came to thinking about how strained financial situations should be handled. Carole wanted to respond to their circumstances by drawing up a strict six-month budget that everyone in the family would agree to adhere to. Having managed her own finances during the many years she'd lived alone, she was accustomed to paying her bills the moment they arrived. She found it hard to tolerate a situation in which the household might remain in arrears from one month to the next one.

Ted didn't see a need for a budget. He saw no reason for the family to go on short-consumption rations. As he continually emphasized during our interview, he'd survived his first wife's alcoholic illness *and* the failure of his business by dint of knowing when and how a debt or loan had to be paid and when it could be staved off for a while.

"I built this house with smoke and mirrors," he said proudly, adding that he was the sole parent who'd been there for his kids, the only person in the world responsible for keeping them clothed, with a roof over their heads. He had been able to keep them in the same schools they'd been attending despite his financial difficulties and his wife's shocking abandonment.

Even as Ted spoke, I could hear his adult children chattering boisterously in the background. The kitchen wall of the Burkes' house sits back-to-back with one of their living-room walls, and his grown daughter and son were in the kitchen, clearly having a good time with one another. I could hear the sounds of pots and dishes clattering, too, and wondered a bit uneasily if they could overhear our conversation. Judging from the expressions on their faces, neither Carole nor Ted had any worries on this score.

Still, the sounds from the kitchen did serve as a continuing reminder of their presence in the household. This was probably why I was suddenly struck by how consistently the couple's discussions of their straitened finances tended to segue into conversations involving these "noncontributing" members of the group. Carol kept gazing at Ted with an irritated, sarcastic expression, as if to remind him that *she* was presently the major earner in the family and the one who'd already contributed a lot of money to the family kitty.

I learned that Ted's daughter, Katie, was in school part-time, and that she had no income at all. His son, Brian, was employed half-time in a liquor store and making unfocused, desultory efforts to find a better job. At some point during the interview, I asked their father straightforwardly if had any concerns about whether his adult children were having trouble separating from home base and striking out on their own independent lives.

Ted responded equably that it was certainly possible that his children were having problems of this sort. Then he added sternly—a message directed more at Carole than at myself—that as far as he was concerned, this was *their home* and had *always been* their home. His kids would most assuredly be welcome to live with him until such time as they were ready to leave and become self-supporting.

In this parent's world, Katie and Brian were his beloved children, and they could remain in the dependent state of childhood as long as they cared to. In his new wife's world, these young adults were noncontributing housemates. It was easy to imagine that each time one of Ted's kids came into the living room, he would feel a sense of affection, interest, and connection. Carole, on the other hand, might feel a twinge of regret or annoyance, because the flow of their intimate and private relationship was being interrupted by these sloppy, unhelpful "housemates." Thus, each member of the pair would experience the multitude of minor events comprising their mutual reality in profoundly different ways and might feel left out or dismayed or betrayed by the way the intimate partner saw things.

As my set of interviews with the Burkes concluded, I did find myself more and more concerned about Ted's ways of handling his finances, which seemed dicey. He appeared to operate according to the dubious principle of staying one short step ahead of his creditors. This was clearly anathema to Carole. I thought, too, about the fact that she'd lent him thirty thousand dollars during their brief, three-month engagement. Would that money ever be returned, or was he conning her, taking advantage of her boundless trust and generosity? The situation was unclear, and as

I drove away, I wondered whether this couple would survive the first five years of their remarriage—in statistical terms, the years of danger and of opportunity.

THE BURKES IN 2010

When I dialed the Burkes' phone number, I wasn't sure that either one of them would be on the other end of the line. Many of the remarried couples whom I'd interviewed in my 1996–97 sample had moved to different houses or elsewhere in the country. Few had left forwarding information, and in many cases, I had no clue about whether their relationships had lasted. But Ted Burke did pick up, after three long, suspenseful rings. "Yes?" he said. His voice had an apprehensive undertone, as if any news that was forthcoming was likely to add to some already existing anxieties.

Thirteen years had passed, and I wasn't sure that he would remember me, but he did, immediately. His voice brightened a bit when he talked about having enjoyed our interviews. I asked him how he and Carole were doing, and he responded in the emotionally neutral tone of voice that I remembered well, "Oh, we split. She left me. She just took off. We're divorced."

I told him that I was sorry to hear it, then asked how long the marriage had lasted. I also asked him what, as he understood it, had brought the ending of the relationship about. Ted answered the first question readily: Carole had departed after about eight months, but they had reconciled after a brief separation. Following that, they'd remained married for another seven months or so, but then she'd left for good and filed for divorce.

It was my second question—What had led to the breakup?—that seemed to give Ted more pause. He cleared his throat and finally said it had probably been due to his children. "She wanted them to pay part of the rent. 'To contribute,' is how she put it," Ted's tone was acid. "But this is my house, and these are my children! I wouldn't hear of it!" His voice had shifted up from its usual neutral gear, and now he sounded indignant. When I said nothing, he repeated, "My own kids!"

"Your kids aren't living with you now, are they?" I asked, for I realized that his children—young adults in the late 1990s—must now be in their thirties. "Oh no," he said. "They're on their own." He drew in a breath as if about to add something more about Katie and Brian, but then said nothing further.

I asked him if he would be willing to meet with me, and he agreed so eagerly that I wondered what his daily life was like at this point in time. Was he feeling somewhat lonesome? Then I asked him how I could reach Carole, and he gave me her telephone number at work—the Yale Child Study Center in New Haven—and her new name, which she had legally changed.

"She now goes by her maiden name, Nowak. It's Polish, or something like that," he said dismissively. He then added, "At one time I did ask her if she wanted to come back, try again, now that the kids are gone. But she wouldn't have any part of it." He was saying that he was the flexible, forgiving partner, yet doing so in a voice as curiously free of affect as I remembered.

I told him that I would interview each of them separately and would call him back to set a time and date.

Later that same afternoon I called Carole Nowak at her office. She sounded glad to hear from me and agreed that she would come to see me in my home office on a Sunday afternoon two weeks hence.

A Bit of a Family

When we sat down for our interview, it took me a while to register the fact that the woman before me was the same Carole Burke I had known some thirteen years earlier. At that time, she had been a slender, taut businesswoman, carefully dressed down to the last gold bracelet and gold-and-onyx earrings. The Carole before me had put on weight and was wearing a boat-necked aqua T-shirt and loose white trousers; no jewelry, no makeup. Something else about her was strikingly different. The fearful, trapped expression had left her face, and she looked peaceful and calm.

I began by asking her about her current job. "It's my impression that you hold a fairly responsible position at the Yale Child Study Center?" It was a question more than a statement.

Carole shrugged, blushed, said that it was no more responsible than any of the previous jobs she'd had, but then she added, "I do think it's an important part of the department."

"What exactly do you do?" I leaned forward in my chair, curious about what her role in that esteemed psychiatric facility might be.

She said that she was now what was known as a certified child and adolescent coordinator. She pushed a lock of reddish brown hair behind her ear. "That is, I'm a person who handles the oversight of training for physicians who want to become skilled in child and adolescent psychiatry. She paused, rolled her eyes, said, "Coming in, I had no idea what the job was. But my boss, a child and adolescent psychiatrist and director of two of the programs, said not to worry. She could teach me everything I needed to know. And she has." Carole's voice was pleased and self-confident.

I said that this sounded like one of the more interesting jobs that she'd had.

She nodded and said amiably, "I think this is my final, forever job. This is where I've taken all of the training that I've had throughout my whole career. This is the place in which it's all being accessed."

"So that must be very satisfying." Again, my statement was also a question.

"I love it," Carole responded simply. "The people at my workplace are exceptionally kind, thoughtful. They are soft-spoken. I have twenty-four doctors for whom I have overall responsibility, and they call me the glue that holds the department together."

She went on to explain that some of her trainees were physicians who had completed their training in adult psychiatry and wanted to take additional training to become board certified in the field of child psychiatry. Others were residents who came directly from medical school and opted for an integrated adult and child psychiatry track.

"Then I suppose there is a turnover—people who graduate from the program?" I asked.

"Yes, every two years I graduate six, seven, or eight." Her voice sounded proud and proprietary. "And every July a bunch of new candidates come in. We consider ourselves the Child Study Center family. And once you become part of this, you're always a part of our family, even if you go off and do something else.

"Psychiatry is not that large a field, and especially child psychiatry, so child psychiatrists get together a couple of times a year for conferences. The faculty who are doing the training and those who are enrolled in one of the programs—all of us—we get together and hear papers, and talk. We're very active in the national group. This is part of my life."

"It sounds fascinating," I said, speaking truthfully.

"It's part of my life," repeated Carole. "It's like having a bit of a family," she added happily.

I Never Felt That Anything Was Ours; It Was His

When I asked Carole how long her marriage to Ted had lasted in the legal sense, she told me that it had been two and a half years, adding that throughout that entire period, she had felt bewildered and impotent. She had never achieved a sense of inclusion—a feeling of belonging in the Burke family household.

"It isn't that there weren't any good times; there were. But I never felt like anything was *ours*. Somehow everything was his, and he was making a little space for me. That's why I wanted him to sell the house and for me to sell my condo. I kept saying that we should get a new place as soon as possible—one that was big enough for both of us, and for the kids if they wanted to come and stay. But I hadn't expected to remain in that house and have them live with us forever. Ted couldn't think beyond that, couldn't realize that they were really grown up."

I recalled how proudly Ted had described himself as the father and provider for his dependent offspring. Perhaps this was a core identity, one he had not been able to part with, for he hadn't seemed to envision a future time in which Katie and Brian would become self-sufficient adults and go off to make lives of their own. Even as this thought crossed my mind, it was accompanied by the mental image of a former time. I flashed upon the picture of a house occupied by the biologically connected Burkes with outsider Carole banging on the door to gain entry.

At the time of our initial interviews, nobody had been responding to any of her requests, and the Burke family was going on with its life as usual. The kitchen was being cared for as nonchalantly as ever—a disturbing problem for Carole that her new spouse kept assuring her was of no real consequence. Ted was telling her that only her own misguided way of thinking was turning it into an issue.

After a short pause, I said, "I could see your struggle to incorporate yourself in Ted's family when I visited. You were working so hard to be heard." Carole shook her head back and forth vigorously, as if to shake off the memory of that time. Then, in a seeming non sequitur, she told me that in the wake of that marriage she would find it hard to put her trust in any man. "Aside from my brother, that is," she amended. Then she laughed, added lightly, "What I tell people now is that the only man—male, I mean—in my life is my cat. He's twenty years old, and he's gone through that whole terrible time with me." She shuddered and fell silent for a few moments.

Lies upon Lies

Carole told me that she had met Ted at a dinner dance for singles. He had danced with her for most of the evening and had told her that he was a policeman. Since she had recently dated someone from the police department, she felt that this was someone she would not have to worry about. Also, Ted was a local person; he lived near Pitney Bowes, the corporation where she worked.

"He was polite, nice-looking, and attentive, so after that evening, we started to go out, and we just talked and talked about all kinds of things. How long had we lived in the area. Where we had gone to school. What were our families were like." Carole folded her hands in schoolgirl fashion, drew them up to her chest. "Later on, I was to learn that much of what he was telling me was completely untrue.

"For instance, he was *not* a policeman. He was something called a supernumerary, which is basically a rental security person. He'd told me that he owned his own home. He didn't; it belonged to his brother. He said that he owned his own business, a private business—"

"Wasn't that a transportation company of some sort?" I interrupted her, recalling our earlier interviews.

She nodded. "He didn't tell me much about that business initially, and later on it turned out that he drove a school bus. He didn't even own the bus; it belonged to his mother. On the marriage license it said that he had been married once before, but some old friends of his started telling me that I was his third wife." She gave me a shamefaced look and shook her head as if to say, "How gullible can you be?" "I kept telling myself, 'Oh no, he wouldn't lie to me.'"

Eventually, though, there had come a time when Carole felt compelled to confront him directly. "I said, 'Ted, people are telling me you're not a real policeman; you're a supernumerary.' But he denied it to my face, said the stories I was hearing were untrue. He said they were completely crazy."

She squeezed her folded hands together so tightly that the knuckles turned white. "Looking back, I think what happened was that I went into that relationship trusting him heart and soul. I believed this was going to be my new life, and I suppose I stopped thinking somehow. Even when I couldn't avoid seeing that it was all a maze of lies, I tried to turn my head away and say, 'No, that can't be true.' But the more information I received, the more proof I got that everything he was telling me was a total fabrication."

I said nothing, but wondered at the credulousness of this seasoned corporate businesswoman who would certainly have behaved differently in a company setting. For Carole Nowak, love and marriage had involved putting those important skills— information gathering, objectivity, clear decision-making—to one side.

"Hadn't you loaned him thirty thousand dollars while you were still engaged?" I asked her.

She nodded her assent. "Yes, I gave him that money so that he would feel comfortable, not threatened by me. He didn't have any assets to speak of because his business had fallen on hard times. He'd made it sound like something temporary, just a brief setback that wouldn't last long. But then, Ted was awfully good at telling people the kind of stories they wanted to hear." Carole's expression looked wry as she recalled how naïve and trusting she had been at the height of that romance. Then she said grimly that much worse was to follow with the appearance of the Internal Revenue Service upon the scene.

Smoke and Mirrors

The Burkes had been married in November, and in the months that followed, many feelings of being disregarded by the original family had left Carole feeling stuck on the outside of the system. Also, periodic incidents had made her feel worried and doubtful about Ted's basic truthfulness. However, it was in February, when she customarily filed her income tax returns, that her new spouse's money issues shot to the forefront of all her other concerns.

"What triggered the big trouble was that the time came to file a joint income tax return," said Carole. "I have always sent mine in sometime in February, but Ted told me that he does his return at the last minute. I said that was all right, but that I had an accountant who had been with me a long time. After much back-and-forth, he finally decided that it would be better if we filed as a couple because I had more money and was bringing in a higher salary. So . . ." She stopped speaking and inhaled deeply as if to calm herself. Then, on the exhaled breath, she said, "This was when I discovered that the so-called mortgage payments I'd been making on the house all these months were actually rental payments. Ted's brother actually owned our house!"

Carole's voice trembled. "So then we couldn't take any deductions on the taxes for the interest on the mortgage because the home we were living in didn't actually belong to us."

"Ted had been ice-skating over the truth," I said quietly. "What else did you find out?"

She nodded but didn't respond directly. Instead she said that when she'd realized seriousness of the skeletons in Ted's closet, she had addressed him with a mightily renewed urgency. "I said, 'Look, I need to know what's going on here! I need to know what I've gotten into.'"

Her husband admitted to having sugarcoated the truth and

explained that he hadn't wanted to burden her with all of these "details"—he was afraid that if he'd done so, she wouldn't have married him. After this initial confession, other financial difficulties of Ted's began to emerge: he had stacks of unpaid credit card bills—cards in his own name, his brother's name, and his mother's name. "In short, he was up to his ears in debt and had absolutely no credit at all," Carole said.

She then fell silent, and after a short while, I asked her what she was thinking about.

"Oh, that in going back to that period and reflecting on it, I realize that in effect I ended up losing a decade of my life on that marriage. Before I met Ted, I was comfortable financially, I dated many different people, I was forty pounds lighter and very active physically," she replied.

"Oh Carole, I'm sorry," I said, seeing the stricken expression on her face.

She shook her head as if to say never mind; this was in the past. "When all of this worrying financial information started to come out," she continued, "I was still committed to working things out. I said that my own credit rating was still excellent, so if we did balance transfers from his cards to mine, we could get a low interest rate on a mortgage. I could sell my condo, which I still owned, and we could put the house in my name. Then it would really be ours. But Ted didn't want to have anything to do with *that*." Her tone was sardonic.

"Why not?"

"Possibly because he didn't trust me. And perhaps because there was more debt that I didn't know about. Ted owed the IRS a great deal of money, and in early April, they sent me a letter saying that they were attaching my salary. They were confiscating all of our wages, and they were going to allocate only enough money to us to cover rent and food. I think it was about six hundred dollars a month."

"How much was owed to them?" I asked, feeling as if, like

Alice, I was falling into an ever-deeper hole as this tale of obfuscation and deceit emerged.

Carole said that the figure was something like a quarter of a million dollars. Before that letter from the IRS arrived, Ted had engaged a mortgage broker—"I don't know where this person came from," Carole admitted—to look at both their books and help them figure out how they could get the house out of his brother's name and into his own. It was during the session with the mortgage broker that she had first learned of Ted's unpaid debt to the IRS and been instructed that she, as his legal wife, was now equally responsible for repaying it.

"I was made to understand that I had to offer up all my life savings—about ten thousand dollars—and live on this stringent budget doled out by the IRS. I mean, wow, just like that, I found that I was dead broke, completely busted."

Out of a Job

One week later, Pitney Bowes, Carole's employer, instituted massive layoffs, and Carole found herself out of a job. "I was completely panicked, and so I went directly to the IRS to tell them what had happened. To my utter amazement, the agent I spoke to wasn't disturbed by this news at all. He simply said, 'Fine. You've lost your job, and therefore none of this will happen.' My life went from, 'They're taking my savings and putting me on a budget,' to, 'I'm in the clear.' That same agent told me that contrary to what Ted's friend had said, I wasn't responsible for any of his debts because those debts had preceded our marriage." She let out a breath of relief that sounded like a whoosh.

"So Ted's 'mortgage broker' had made you feel that you were on the hot seat?" I asked.

She nodded. "Yes, that I was on the hook for everything."

I nodded, recalling Ted's remark made many years earlier that he'd kept the house and cared for his children using "smoke and mirrors" all along the way. It seemed clear that he had used similar strategies to lure and keep Carole in this marriage.

"Yes," she continued, "but I still maintain that if I was armed with the same information, I'd have been likely to make the same decisions. I just wasn't ever a person who felt that people were out to tell lies, that they weren't to be trusted."

"You were trusting to a T, in other words," I smiled.

"You could call it S for stupid," said Carole, her cheeks flushing.

Then she told me that after filing tax returns in mid-April, she and Ted had separated. She moved out of his house and began living with a widowed aunt who resided in a nearby town.

Persona and Person

The Burkes' separation had lasted no longer than a couple of months. Carole's aunt was a devoutly religious woman who kept counseling her to return to her marriage and do her best to work things out. Her own parents and other members of her strongly Catholic family were echoing these sentiments, dwelling on the sanctity of her marital vows. At the same time, Ted was telephoning her frequently with promises that certain household irritants would be removed and that he would be a different person as far as dealing with their finances was concerned. He swore that his behavior would change and that she could now trust him completely.

"Ted is a fantastic actor," Carole said drily. "He wasn't ever being truthful. He wasn't being honest. I just didn't understand that." Like any other believable actor, Ted could speak his lines with ardor and resonance even when they had no correspondence with his inner reality.

After a while, believing in his protestations, she moved back into the Burke household. The active, energetic Carole soon had a full-time job working for a company called Executone. She also had a part-time job as a jewelry saleswoman and was taking courses at a nearby state college in order to complete her unfinished college degree. The family was on its way to getting its shaky finances under control. Ted's astronomical credit card balances had been transferred to Carole's card, and because her own credit standing was excellent, they were able to work at paying down their "mutual" debt on far less demanding terms.

At this point in his life, Ted Burke had no credit eligibility of his own and therefore was unable to continue his wanton credit card borrowing.

A New Role Model

In the Peter Pan atmosphere that pervaded the Burke household, Ted's offspring were not given to imagining a future in which they might operate as self-sufficient adults. Carole's entry into the family had inevitably disturbed its lethargic atmosphere, for her very presence provided a vision of initiative and focus. For Katie and Brian, children of a failed, phlegmatic father and a runaway, alcoholic mother, this new stepparent was to become a role model, revealing a hitherto unimagined, alternative way of being.

When she returned to the household, Brian was still working at a liquor store at night and playing video games in his room during much of the rest of his waking hours. Katie, who had dropped out of school, was working for a florist and going out on wild drinking sprees most evenings. But below the radar of her own realization, Carole's active presence was affecting the stalemated existence in which her young "roommates" were entrapped.

"It's hard to tell when it happened, but over time they began to take my way of being very seriously," Carole recounted. "Remember, Katie was only fourteen when her mother left, so she was in that adolescent phase. She didn't know what a woman's role was supposed to be, since she had a mother who was dysfunctional. Before coming to know me, she'd never realized that as a female, she had options. When she saw that I was going to school and that I was holding down a successful job, she understood that getting an education was the key."

Within months after Carole's arrival, Katie applied for entry to the same college her stepmother was attending. She also took out student loans while continuing to work at the florist shop part-time. "I truly believe my role modeling was the impetus to getting her focused," Carole said, with pride in her voice. Then she added with an amused smile, "We used to do our homework together on Sunday evenings."

Her effect on Brian came about more slowly. "There were times when the two of us would be alone in the house or when we would be cooking in the kitchen. Brian liked cooking. And while we worked, I would talk to him about his future. I would say, 'You are so talented when it comes to working with electronics. Why don't you get some serious training and put that capability to use?' I kept trying to project his field of vision into the future by asking him, 'Where do you want to be when you're fifty years old? Do you want to be a clerk in a liquor store? Do you want to be as adrift as your father is?'"

"So you were letting Ted's kids know that he was no role model?" I commented.

"Oh, they knew it." Carole shrugged. "What I kept saying to them was, 'There are alternatives.'" Eventually, she told me, Brian went to a well-regarded local trade school, and as a result he now had a high-paying job as a computer electronics expert in a large corporation. He was happily married and had a young family. Katie had taken teacher training classes and was now an elementary school teacher, the wife of a veterinarian, and the mother of a new baby.

"By the way, she has cut off relations with her father completely," Carole said. "It was a toxic environment, and I believe the kids didn't realize how toxic it was until they actually got out of it." Still, she and Katie had remained in very close touch. These days they shared a loving, quasi-mother/daughter relationship.

Although her sojourn in the Burke household had been a relatively brief one, Carole's influence had actually been transformative for both of Ted's aimless, motherless children. Even though the marriage itself had been a failure, this stepparent had actually become the family's ultimate insider.

Matters of the Heart

"I think of myself as very rational, logical person," said Carole, "except where matters of the heart are concerned. There, I am still rational and logical, but I let my heart take the front-row seat." In her second tour of duty as Ted's wife, she hadn't found life any easier. She became aware that he was drinking heavily, not only publicly but behind closed doors.

"I guess the final straw had to do with the drinking. He knew how much that bothered me. I kept finding these empty bottles of vodka stashed around the house, and one time I got upset and took a bottle and poured it right down the sink, right in front of him. He was livid. At that point we stopped talking to each other."

Carole was soon feeling abandoned and desolate. "I felt trapped, like a cornered animal. I couldn't afford to do anything because we were so deeply in debt, and the debt was in *my* name. I couldn't tell my parents, because they would never have supported a divorce. They would say I had to try harder, that I was too strong a person." There was no support coming from anywhere. Carole was sleepless, anxious, and experiencing attacks of unalloyed panic.

One day she came into her office looking so distraught that her coworkers told her that she should leave immediately and get herself checked at a nearby medical clinic. "As soon as I saw the doctor at that clinic, he recognized what was happening to me. I was put on an antidepressant—Zoloft, I think—and they referred me to a psychiatrist."

It was in the course of her therapeutic treatment that Carole realized she'd never be able to change Ted. She could not fix the situation, and the sooner she managed to get out of it, the better it was going to be for her. Her heart was long gone from the front-row seat that it had occupied earlier in the relationship.

Within weeks, Carole moved out of the Burke house on an afternoon when she knew that Ted would be away. "The only thing I took with me were all the bills. I left everything else, knowing I could come back for my clothes and furniture, but that if I didn't take these papers and his checking account I would never get to know the full story of what had been going on."

She was to spend the following months poring over these documents. Impoverished by their joint debts, she was living with her godmother, having put her furniture and much of her clothing in storage. "When the divorce hearing finally arrived, I marched into the courtroom with a roll-along suitcase filled with these three-inch binders." She had spent the year documenting every single financial transaction; it been a long line to trace backward in time, a work of serious fiscal archaeology. "In the end, I got everything laid out clearly on the courtroom table," she said.

The judge ruled that Ted had to repay all of the money owed to his ex-wife in a series of monthly installments. "Actually, the majority of these payments were for purchases that had been made before I even existed in his life," she said. "The decision was that he would pay me a certain amount every month, and at the end of that period, he would come up with a balloon payment amounting to twelve thousand dollars."

After that, on the basis of this court judgment, she had obtained a bank installment loan of thirty-five thousand dollars and paid off every one of the credit cards. After most of a decade, the status quo ante—Carole's financial standing before the marriage—was finally restored.

It Was God's Plan

It is hard to tease out truth from fiction when one is in the presence of an accomplished liar like Ted Burke. This is especially true when someone is hopelessly in the grip of a romantic myth to the effect that, "The man I love can't be deceptive. I love him. I know him. He's a good person, and he loves me." It was this fantasy that had transformed Carole from a woman of independent means to a debt-ridden pauper within a remarkably brief period of time. Restoring herself to her previous independent, credit-worthy way of being in the world had swallowed up an entire decade of her life.

But in some ways, she felt fortunate. For example, it was through that doomed relationship with Ted that she had come to know and love his daughter, Katie—and then Katie's husband and her child. "Katie is the reason I met my ex-husband. God decided that she needed to be part of my life, and there is no other way for Katie to have come into my life without going through Ted. He served that purpose, but we both left him behind," Carole said.

Another, earlier example of her "good fortune," or what she felt to be the guiding hand of God, was the fact that Pitney Bowes had had the massive layoffs, which had led to her consultation with the IRS agent. It was by means of that happy chance that she'd learned that she was in no way responsible for debts Ted had incurred before her marriage to him.

"There is a spirit," said Carole earnestly, in going over these events. "There is something beyond what we see and hear. It's a kind of impetus or voice that—when you come to a fork in the road—whispers to you, 'Take this path.'" Despite all that had happened to her, Carole believed in her good luck and the presence of a benevolent deity.

A Financial HIV Test

I asked Carole what advice she would give to other remarrying individuals, particularly those coming into a stepparenting situation.

There was a long silence; she didn't seem to have an answer at hand. At last she said, choosing her words carefully, "Coming in as the childless person that I was, I would probably not be as generous and all-giving. I tend to want to share everything, to make everybody's life as full and rich and comfortable as I can. But I can exhaust my own resources in this way." Her voice trailed off.

I thought of the thirty-thousand-dollar loan to Ted she had made during their engagement. Why hadn't she insisted that it be secured in some way, put into an escrow account? Why hadn't the request itself set some alarm bells ringing?

"You certainly did exhaust your resources, big time," I commented.

"I did. So the advice I would give would be to take everything slowly. We didn't have a prenuptial agreement, which would probably be a good idea in general. Then everyone would be compelled to lay their cards on the table. Is there credit card debt? Does the person actually own his house? What is his job, and what kind of salary is he bringing home? You yourself can be an honest person, but how can you know if the other person's being honest with you?" She raised both her arms in the air as if these questions were coming to me in the form of an entreaty.

"Are you suggesting that couples entering a remarriage should always have a prenup?" I asked her.

She nodded and said that, yes, she would always want the parent's children to know that what their father owed to them would come to them, but that if something happened to break up the couple's new life, the newcomer would be able to stand on her own two feet again. "I'm thinking of the prenup in the same light as the HIV test," she explained. "That you aren't taking it because you think there is a problem; you're taking it to show the other person that you are committed to him or her."

I wasn't quite sure what she meant, so, in an effort to clarify her meaning, I said, "Taking the HIV test does involve letting the partner know that this is a safe step for her or him to be taking. It means letting the new spouse know that he or she isn't going to go to the doctor one day and discover that he or she has caught HIV."

Carole took this in, but shook her head and said, "That's true, but my own idea about the prenup is that it says 'I want you to know that I am being honest with you about my life, my home, my occupation, my financial affairs. That I am being truthful with you in all these respects. That there are no secrets, and I'm really the same person I've managed to convince you that I am.'"

CHAPTER SEVEN

Wedding Bells and Dollar Bills

One of the most taboo words among couples contemplating remarriage is the "M" word—that is, money. It is all too easy to picture the two lovers sharing a romantic dinner, luxuriating in good food, wine, and each other's company. After a long dry spell of seeking a new relationship where the chemistry is "right" (they've been enjoying the best sex they've had in years), the pair have found they share the same values, sense of humor, and plea- sure in spending time together. Everything seems to be working.

But if the woman (say, a divorcée with two daughters, seven and nine) is looking across the table and wondering about her prospective mate's financial status, dare she come right out and ask about it? Can she suggest a quiet evening during which they share their financial spreadsheets and discuss the ways in which they'll manage their merging household's resources? Would her partner-to-be (also divorced and the father of two older children) start to look at her askance? If he is still feeling bruised by the financial beating he took during the divorce proceedings, will he begin to wonder if this marvelous new partner is just another greedy female who's more interested in his income and assets than she is in him as a person? She may fear (and rightly so) that such questions would shatter the wonderful mood in which they'd been enveloped.

Deep-seated misgivings like these often lead to a situation in which vital questions about money are never asked and therefore remain unanswered when the remarriage vows are spoken. However, there is a great deal of information that the remarrying partners need to exchange, lest some unpleasant surprises rear up at a later date. To take a simple example, what is known about the new love's "money personality"? One member of the pair of may be awash in credit card debt and feel perfectly comfortable paying the minimum balance due each month, while the other is horrified by anything less than paying the entire credit card balance as soon as the bill arrives. An extreme example of this divergence of money habits was certainly seen in the calamitous story of the Burkes.

According to Margorie Engel, former president of the Stepfamily Association of America (SAA), remarrying couples often bring not only sharply divergent attitudes about money into the relationship, but also baggage from their former lives. "For instance, people generally assume that the new spouse is the beneficiary of the mate's life insurance policy. In second marriages, not so; in fact, it's very seldom so unless an entirely new policy has been taken out at a much greater premium due to increased age and possibly new medical issues as well," she told me in the course of several wide-ranging conversations.

Much more frequently it is the ex-spouse who is the beneficiary of the policy, because it has already been attached in a divorce agreement as assurance for child and spousal support payments. "However, when you are newly remarried and facing the mountain of changes in front of you—finding a place to live; taking on the care of extra children; dealing with more automobiles and the added insurance expenses that go along with that, et cetera—obtaining a new life insurance policy is simply not going to be high on your list," said Engel, whose area of expertise is remarriage finances. "Nevertheless, being the beneficiary of your husband's life insurance policy is a benchmark of financial security for many women."

In actuality, unknown to everyone involved, the new wife may not be provided for in any way if a sudden crisis occurs. It is only after her partner's biological children reach the age of eighteen and his child support payments come to an end that the money is no longer needed for assurance purposes. At this point, the remarried mate may be named the new beneficiary of her husband's policy. "That is," remarked Engel drily, "if either person in the remarriage happens to think about it."

Another unpleasant surprise may come in the guise of lost college tuition assistance. Every bit of tuition help of any kind—be it a dependent child's scholarship or grant or work-study plan—begins with filling out the Free Application for Federal Student Aid (FAFSA) form. If, say, a single parent is earning $35,000 a year, and she remarries a man who is making $90,000 a year, the new husband's income is counted as part of the houschold's annual income—even if he is not contributing a nickel to his stepchild's education. In fact, Engel told me that her oldest daughter's scholarship was revoked the semester after her own remarriage at the age of forty.

In one interesting instance, a couple whom I interviewed said they had cohabited for six years in order to avoid declaring the stepfather's income on an FAFSA document. The presumptive stepdad's position was that he had put his own three children through college and did not want to assume responsibility for underwriting the son of his second wife. Engel's own view of this strategy is somewhat negative due to her concern about the example it sets for the maturing children who are involved.

A remarrying woman surely needs to be aware that when she says, "I do," to her new spouse, she will be losing the right to collect benefits on her former mate's social security record. If she had remained single and her first marriage had lasted more than ten years, she would have been eligible (at age sixty-two) to receive spousal benefits from her retiring husband's social security stipend. Interestingly enough, if the woman's subsequent marriage were to end by death, divorce, or annulment, she can then become reinstated as a beneficiary of her original spouse and can receive benefits on his social security account. Moreover, if her first spouse is now deceased and her remarriage has ended (by divorce, annulment, or death), she can actually qualify as her original husband's widow and receive spousal benefits without affecting the benefits of his other survivors. Strange as it seems, two widows can be collecting on the same man's social security account simultaneously.

A SEA OF DOCUMENTS

While many couples on the eve of remarriage are quite comfortable discussing their sexual histories openly, the very idea of initiating a conversation about the state of their finances is fraught with feelings of intimidation and embarrassment. However, no conversation is more important when it comes to establishing a trusting, safe relationship. As Engel puts it, each mate needs to be secure in the answer to the question: "What happens to me if something happens to you?" A full disclosure of each partner's financial identity is the best wedding gift the two could possibly give to one another.

Ideally speaking, what are the documents they need to share in order to fully understand one another's financial standing? A comprehensive list appears in an article—one among a series of informative essays—that Engel has posted on the SAA website. It includes such categories as: "Credit card list; Household inventory and appraisals; Personal banking; Money lent to others; Money borrowed from others; Investments, including applications (e.g., for a bank loan) and a financial statement (bank account and stocks owned, etc.); Medical insurance; Life insurance; Personal property insurance; Tax returns; Employment history/resume; Employer policies/benefits; Retirement dollars;

Income records, and (if it pertains) proprietorship or partnership in a family-owned business."

Whew, this annotated checklist is long enough to take your breath away! And Engel suggests still other topics that should be raised in a premarital discussion due to their potential financial impact upon the pair. High on this new list are such issues as tax problems, needy children of all ages, looming college expenses, shaky job security, and extended family demands—an aging, ill parent, for example. As Engel warns, "Splintered loyalties, new responsibilities, and changing needs all force remarried couples to take into consideration the makeup of this new and complicated family."

Of course there are often circumstances that are specific to a particular couple's situation, as Engel is quick to note. Matters such as a lack of maintenance on a house or auto or appliances that may soon require attention will be part of a potential partner's overall financial picture. So will a "time-bomb" health problem and any benefits that will have to be surrendered at the time of the remarriage—social security, mentioned above, or perhaps a job or a pension.

At the very least, asserts Engel, couples need to have discussions about certain key topics, such as each partner's money management style; one person's move away from his or her home state, quitting a job and seeking another one in a new locale; regular and irregular income sources; diagnosed health or emotional problems; inheritance money; retirement security; and health care proxies and wills. A key question to be asked and answered is whether the pair will want to have children together. This can become an important issue in a situation where, for instance, a man in his fifties who has already raised one family marries a woman in her thirties who yearns to start another—much to her presumptive spouse's chagrin.

NET WORTH AND RISK MANAGEMENT

As financial expert Joanna Bickel pointed out to me, Engel's long list might seem dizzying at first, but it boils down to a statement about what the person *owns* and what he or she *owes*: "That is a net worth statement. It includes bank accounts, stock investments, retirement pensions, et cetera; and of course, credit card debt and other bills outstanding."

An individual's financial identity is determined by this net worth statement, Bickel said. "If you sit down and go through the entire list, you will get to the partnership in the family business and the fifty-thousand-dollar loan you still owe to Aunt Tillie." And at the end of this process, you will have created a financial statement.

The insurance part of Engel's list—medical insurance, automobile insurance, and so forth—falls into another category, risk management, explained Bickel. "This has to do with all the 'what ifs'—all of the awful, unexpected things that can happen. Here you would want to know how an intended mate is spending his or her money to protect against serious property damage or illness or a disability of some kind." Romance is wonderful, but marriage involves not only an emotional but an economic transaction.

However, as Engel, Bickel, Papernow, and other stepfamily experts I've consulted agree, an open, detailed conversation about each partner's financial position occurs in only a minority of remarriages prior to the ceremony. What a difference this would have made in the case of the Burkes! As I reflected about them, I could not help but wonder why a warning bell had not gone off in Carole's head when Ted asked her for a loan of thirty thousand dollars during the period of their engagement. Why hadn't it occurred to her that this meant he couldn't qualify for a bank loan—and that this could be just the tip of a disastrous financial iceberg? Had she been more anxious to stay positive and get married than to pause and think things through before leaping into that disastrous situation?

THE MARITAL BALANCE SHEET

Some couples, when they remarry, simply pool all their financial resources together. This is the so-called "one-pot" solution to managing the new household's money. Other partners decide to keep separate accounts and handle all child-rearing and household expenses on a fifty-fifty basis. Obviously, this is a "two-pot" arrangement. A third way of managing stepfamily finances—and this is the one Papernow favors—is the "three-pot" method. This arrangement calls for each member of the pair to handle personal expenses plus those of the children he or she has brought to the marriage, while both contribute to a third account that is used for the upkeep of the whole family (food, mortgage payments, repairs, insurance, and the like).

A number of researchers have tried to ferret out an answer to the question: Which of these styles of money management is the best? Does one of them lead to more family happiness and a greater sense of contentment? The answer appears to be a clear-cut no. There is no one financial model that is guaranteed to work better than the others.

Interestingly enough, it has been established that money is the major source of conflict in first-marriage couples, and arguments about children come in second. That situation is turned on its head when it comes to subsequent marriages: remarried couples' fights are mostly about children; money quarrels come in at second place. This isn't meant to gainsay the fact that financial matters do carry a significant symbolic freight in stepfamily households. As Engel wisely observes in one of her highly informative SAA articles, "Trust, commitment, and the guarantee of permanence are the underlying issues."

Although remarried partners typically decide upon one or another of the one-, two-, or three-pot solutions, they nevertheless tend to create their own variations on these basic themes. For example, a couple who has agreed on three money pots—mine, yours, and ours—will have to take into account the basic fairness of the plan. As Engel told me, "The agreement may be that she takes care of her kids' needs and he takes care of his kids' needs. But if they are going fifty-fifty for the household expenses and she makes $40,000 a year and he makes $100,000 a year, the couple is going to have to make an adjustment for that discrepancy." The marital balance sheet has to produce a situation of even-handedness.

A perennial difficulty is that many men don't have a clue about what it costs to rear children, observed Engel. "They may know about the big things, such as the orthodontist and school tuition, but they're not aware of the day-to-day expenses, such as buying small items like Band-Aids and toothpaste or having an all-day birthday party or taking the husband's daughter out to help her buy a prom dress. Women have repeatedly told me that they are afraid to ask for reimbursement and that their spouses have no idea how much of their own money they end up spending." These daily cash bites are, relatively speaking, mosquitoes, but they can become an elephant in the room fairly quickly.

As Engel pointed out, there are instances in which a working woman remarries a man with young children in his care (perhaps a widower) and then leaves her job to create a welcoming home environment and take care of the new household. In such circumstances, she is likely to be giving up whatever retirement remuneration she's amassed up to that point. "If she stays home and gets the house made pretty and comfortable and all of the children resettled, she is not taking care of her own personal financial security," said the expert. In the interests of the marital balance sheet, the partners must make some adjustments in order to create a situation of equity. However, in many cases, this reality has not crossed the mind of either partner before the ring is on the new bride's hand, and by that point, it may have become impossible for any such adjustment to be made. An outstanding instance of this sort was cited in a 1998 research investigation published by Engel. In this study, 426 remarried wives reported on how they viewed their current financial position. One respondent, a PhD, sent in this blistering statement: "If I could start this marriage over, I would never leave my sixty-plus-K job, dump my house, roll out (of state), meet the stepchild from hell, and watch this entire marriage go down the toilet as the stepchild smiles with satisfaction."

But at the other end of the response spectrum (which was classified in the categories Good, Fair, or Poor), the Engel researchers received replies that sounded more like this: "I wouldn't change anything. I think we have done a good job with it. Helps to have some money to work with and to have similar goals and 'money sense.' We have spent hours and hours on this area of our marriage."

One must suspect that the first respondent's eyes had been so clouded by romantic feelings and high expectations that she'd been temporarily blind to the possible consequences of the radical decisions she was making. It is easy to imagine that during this disillusioned woman's courtship and engagement, the "M" word was not ever mentioned.

INHERITANCE ISSUES

If the courting or newly remarried couple has been shying away from wide-ranging financial discussions, they've probably allowed questions about inheritance to fall into a state of benign neglect. What, then, will happen if the higher-earning spouse— often the husband—perishes in an auto accident or suffers a fatal heart attack a couple of years after the wedding? If there is no prenuptial arrangement and no will has been drawn up, the way he would have wished to dispose of his estate will be unknown. In this moment of crisis, does the new wife stand to inherit any of her late spouse's assets?

I put this question to Leslie E. Grodd, a lawyer who has worked in the area of trusts and estates for forty-three years and is listed among the best lawyers in America. He said that family law differs from state to state, but in Connecticut, where he practices, the remarried wife would inherit the first $100,000 from the estate and then share the rest of the estate equally with any surviving biological children. If the deceased mate had no children but had living parents, a somewhat similar distribution of assets would obtain. The first $100,000 would go to the new wife, and she would also receive 75 percent of her late husband's estate; the remaining 25 percent would go to his parents. In brief, the state of Connecticut (like other states) has established a default prenuptial agreement in the absence of a real will.

But can the surviving wife continue to live in the comfortable home that belongs to him and to which she has moved, along with her school-age son, after selling her condo? Is her name even on the mortgage? No one wants to discover the answers to such questions in the midst of a catastrophe.

Also, from the point of view of a remarried person's potential blood-related heirs, the remarried spouse's presence on the scene, no matter how fondly they view him or her, can create an antagonistic situation. For example, one Massachusetts couple told me that when the husband's father died, his second wife (the man's stepmother) lived on in the house the pair had inhabited. Although the son had been told that he and his children were remembered in his dad's will, it was never filed legally and could not be found anywhere. In this instance, the assets of the estate did not follow the bloodline but were eventually left to the stepmother's niece. This is a highly atypical outcome, because both the remarried spouse and the biological children are usually beneficiaries of the estate.

Retired Massachusetts probate and family court judge E.

Chouteau Levine explained to me how this could happen. In this particular case, most of the father's wealth had been tied up in the large home that he owned jointly with his remarried spouse. If, as in this instance, there is joint ownership of the house, the surviving mate inherits outright, and the home is outside the probate court's jurisdiction. It is never part of the estate that would be divided up by the stepparent and the decedent's biological children. While the father may have instructed his second wife to leave the house to his son, she was within her rights to leave it to whomever she pleased.

As Levine told me, "Everything depends upon how the property is held. If it is held 'in common,' the home would have been handled by the probate court as part of the decedent's estate. If it is 'jointly owned' by the remarried couple, the surviving spouse owns it outright. If the father, in this instance, had truly meant to pass his assets to his son eventually, he ought to have educated himself about the nature of family law." If he, like many people, had drifted along and simply expected his spouse to "do the right thing," he was being somewhat naïve; she was free to ignore his wishes because the home was now hers. And as sole owner, were she to die intestate, the property would not pass to a stepchild but to a blood-related relative of her own.

The clear moral of this story is that both parties to a remarriage must become familiar with family law in general and the way in which their state decides inheritance matters in particular. This information can be found by reading the state statutes in a local library, visiting a family-law clinic at a law school, or asking a trusts and estates lawyer like Leslie Grodd or a probate court officer like Chouteau Levine to spell out this very pertinent information. The essential bottom line here is that a legally enforceable will, trust, or prenuptial agreement is needed in order to ensure that a dying person's true intentions are carried out. So it is worth reiterating once again that no sensible planning for the future can ever occur if the "M" word remains unspoken.

BROACHING THE MONEY DISCUSSION

Although experts in the field agree that the exchange of clear, accurate financial information *before* remarriage can defuse anxieties and uncover potential problems, few presumptive partners know how to get this conversation started. There is so much fear of pricking the bubble of romance by sounding untrusting or greedy or needlessly intrusive. Yet a money discussion, preferably in the presence of a disinterested third party, such as a lawyer, financial counselor, or tax accountant, should be in the forefront of every remarrying couple's thinking. So how in the world is one to get such a coolly clinical-sounding discussion started? Are there safe ways to broach so tricky a topic?

One way of approaching the matter might be to take a roundabout route. The partner who wants to open the conversation might begin by asking the other partner about his or her general expectations going forward. Does he or she give the children an allowance, and if so, how much is it? And how shall we handle the child support payments I receive? What about the rental on the condo that I used to live in? When outside money of my own arrives, should it be spent on myself and my children, or should it go into our family pot? Are we going to have one checking account with both our names on it, and if so, what is that to pay for?

A general talk about how money matters will be handled in the future can segue naturally into a conversation about the financial resources currently available (savings, bank accounts, brokerage accounts, real estate, and so on). Of course it hardly needs saying that it's best to see the documents that support the statements each member of pair is making when one considers that Ted Burke was lying to his fiancée about practically everything. Carole Burke was led to believe she was paying the mortgage payments on their own house, though Ted's brother was the actual proprietor.

Another, more direct procedure might be along these lines: "Say, you know I went out to dinner with a few of my colleagues, a couple of who are remarried. And they suggested very strongly that we two should have a long talk about our finances so that we're completely clear about what each of us is bringing to the household kitty and how we think our expenses should be handled."

A third, somewhat similar opening might sound like this: "I hope you don't mind my raising a somewhat sensitive issue, but when you and I started getting serious, I began reading some articles posted on the National Stepfamily Resource Center." Here it should be noted that the Stepfamily Association of America has been absorbed into the National Stepfamily Resource Center (NSRC), and Engel's helpful articles can be easily found in the archives of the new Web site.

Finally, a somewhat more lighthearted yet safe way of introducing a financial discussion would be to say, "I know this can be a thorny subject, so let's start by making a list of what we each think is involved in the topic of money. Let's name the ones that would be the hardest for us to handle. Which ones are the easiest? Then let's knock off the easy ones immediately. Of the more difficult ones, which would it be the least troubling for us to get started on?" I like this approach because it allows each partner a certain latitude for thinking things out and also has the feeling of a game. Nevertheless, it must be emphasized that any agreements reached may be meaningless unless they are documented in a letter and witnessed by a notary.

Overall, the very best way of putting the matter of finances to rest is in the company of that third disinterested party mentioned above, if the couple has the wherewithal to afford these professional services. But however it happens, remarrying couples should never be shy about discussing what money they are bringing to the new relationship, what money has been promised elsewhere (such as on an insurance policy), how they plan to handle their mutual finances in the future, and what arrangements have been made in the event of a disabling illness or the death of one of them.

One or both of them will typically have come to the remarriage with some resources and/or obligations from the past, and they must collaborate to work out a viable, fair system when it comes to the running of the household, as well as a plan for whatever unknowns may occur in the future.

CHAPTER EIGHT

Across Cultures:
Miguel Perez and Vicki de Matteo,
2010

Miguel Perez and Vicki de Matteo had been married for five years at the time of our interviews. Technically speaking, this was a first marriage for both of them, but since Vicki had brought her very young, out-of-wedlock daughter Christina into the relationship, it was virtually indistinguishable from a remarriage and had had a stepfamily structure from the outset.

Miguel was a first-generation Puerto Rican, and Vicki was part of a much more assimilated, close-knit Italian-American family. This meant that the pair was likely to confront not only some of the challenges described in the architectural model (insider/outsider issues, disparate family cultures, parenting tasks, and so on), but also the widely differing values and assumptions routinely prevalent in the ethnic groups from which they sprang.

Miguel, a construction worker, was of medium height, compact, well muscled, and hard as flint. He had a mocha complexion, dark eyes, and a head of soft brown hair. There was something sweet, cautious, and hesitant about him. Vicki, a physician's assistant, worked for a doctor at a local hospital. She was far from uncertain and often answered questions posed to Miguel at moments when he seemed to be having difficulty expressing himself.

Vicki was thirty-five, two years older than Miguel, and seemed to take a maternal, watchful attitude toward him. They were parents of a mutual child, Anthony, now five years old. Had that pregnancy been the reason for the marriage? I wondered. I knew that Miguel and Vicki had been living together since Vicki's daughter, Christina, now sixteen, had been a little over four years old. Chrissie's biological father was an alcoholic—someone who had spent time in jail for multiple drunk-driving incidents. He was making only sporadic contact with his child at this time. Miguel, as a stepparent, was the only reliable male figure who had been present throughout Christina's childhood years.

I asked him if he'd had qualms about marrying a woman with a child. Before he could respond, Vicki burst in. "I thought I'd be alone, for always! My own belief—me being a woman with a child—was that I would never meet someone who would want to be with me and take my kid into the bargain. That's just baggage."

Miguel smiled and said his friends had kept saying, "You're going out with a girl with a kid? That's going to be nothing but problems."

"So you think that people thought he was nutty to be getting involved with you?" I asked Vicki.

"Yeah," she said, and then I posed the same question to Miguel.

"I think what she thinks," he replied. "That people were saying, 'Wow, this guy is carrying someone else's luggage.'"

I asked him if he himself felt that way. He shook his head, said, "No, no, not a bit."

Here Vicki intervened quickly. "Because I made sure of that," she said. "I didn't want to push my daughter on him. I took charge of her as *mine*. I never wanted him to feel like he had the responsibility to raise her, even though he was getting it, no matter what." She was clear about never wanting Miguel to be too involved in her daughter's parenting.

Vicki, a tall, shapely woman with deeply set green eyes and shoulder-length dark hair, spoke in the firm, authoritative voice of a health professional. I asked her how had she managed to raise Christina while keeping Miguel apart and separate, since they were all living in the same house.

"I tried to control it," she said, "and maybe I shouldn't have, because that's probably why they're not very close, even after all these years." A cloud of uncertainty crossed her face but was gone in a moment. "I never pushed her on him," she declared. "I worked it so that she always had to come to me. It was always, 'You ask *me*; Mommy will do it for you; You come to Mommy.' I didn't want to inconvenience him. And I did a lot of that while she was growing up."

I asked Miguel whether he had wanted it that way. He was silent for a moment, and I thought he wouldn't answer. But then he said, "In the beginning, I thought she was keeping the kid away because the two of us were so young when we got together, and I guess we weren't sure which direction we'd be going in. Were we going to stay together or a couple or would we separate? I figured Vicki didn't want another person to get attached to Chrissie—someone who might not be there in the long run."

"Would that have been your own preference, to keep your distance? Or would you have liked to have a closer, more involved relationship with your stepdaughter?" I asked him.

Miguel met my gaze directly and said, "Yes, definitely. I would have liked to be closer to Christina."

I smiled, said, "At sixteen, it's still possible to make it happen. For instance, couldn't you do some special father-daughter things with her, like take her out to lunch without Vicki being there? Or take her to a show or concert that she wants to go to?" Even as I made this helpful suggestion, I could have bit my tongue, for it was not an interviewer's business or concern.

"Yeah, maybe she will go for that," said Miguel, his voice sounding dubious. He glanced at his wife's impassive expression, and I could see that he was already retreating. "Chrissie's at the point where she's a teenager now. She's into her own friends," he explained, shaking his head to say that it wasn't going to be feasible.

I could see that I had drifted into sensitive waters, and Miguel did not want to rock the boat. In this family, it was an unspoken rule that stepfather and stepdaughter were to be kept in decidedly separate compartments. Vicki was the stuck insider—the person who had access to them both. It was at that early moment that I decided to pose a question that I usually reserved for much later on in the interview: "Miguel, do you feel like an insider or an outsider in this family? Do you feel like you're someone in the center, or do you feel like you're outside it?"

He thought for a moment and then replied, "I would say fifty-fifty. I can't say either one or the other."

"Fifty-fifty," I repeated. "Meaning that you're an insider with your son, Anthony, and Vicki, and an outsider where you and Vicki and Chrissie are concerned?"

He nodded his assent: "Yeah, yeah." I turned to Vicki and asked her the same question. "I'm inside," she responded comfortably. "I'm inside all the way, most definitely." Miguel shifted his position, looking uneasy. It was as if there were two families living inside this couple's house. In one of them, Miguel was an accepted insider, and in the other he was the excluded outsider, who (I suspected) felt his lack of inclusion and influence keenly.

THEN AND NOW

Since Miguel claimed he'd never had a significant love interest in his life before teaming up with Vicki, I addressed the following question to her alone: "What do you think is the major difference between your former relationship and this current one?"

Vicki's entire body seemed to relax back into the sofa cushion, and her eyes took on a faraway expression. "Frank was my first boyfriend that I ever had. Just kids, you know, and we're really in love. He's the father of my daughter." Confusingly enough, she had switched into the present tense. "And also I would say we communicate," she added.

"Yes, I would say 'communicate.' Definitely, we do," said Miguel, misunderstanding which man she was talking about.

Vicki turned to him swiftly, asked, "How would you know?"

"Because we do." He looked taken aback.

"I wasn't talking about you and me. I was talking about *me and Frank,*" she said.

"Oh, I'm sorry, I'm sorry," apologized Miguel. Actually he had nothing to apologize about. It was easy to see why he had gotten mixed up.

"You jumped feet first into the action," I joked, and he laughed and said, "Yep, right in there."

I continued questioning Vicki along the same line: "What had your fantasies been about how this second relationship would differ from the first one? What parts of those fantasies really did come true, and what parts had turned out to be very different from what you'd imagined?"

She turned to Miguel, gazed at him briefly, turned back to me. "My fantasy was that there would be much more communication. A little more authority."

"That Miguel would assume the role of the male in the household?" I asked.

She nodded. "My ex-husband was very passive. Very quiet. Never had an opinion. Never did anything but drink," she said, her voice growing censorious. I was baffled. Hadn't Vicki said that she and Frank had communicated well? Perhaps she'd meant they had done so in the first love-struck period of the relationship.

I asked her if Frank, given his drinking problem, had been able to hold down a job. She nodded her assent and said that her ex-spouse, like Miguel, worked in construction. I then asked her whether there were patterns in that first relationship that she especially *didn't* want to see happen in this one. I also asked her whether there were parts of that earlier relationship she'd like to see preserved or that she missed in any way.

Vicki shook her head. "Miss the past? No, not at all. Except maybe Frank's family. His mother, most of all. I remained very close to her until she passed away," she said, as a cloud passed across her mobile features. "As for the patterns I wanted to see changed," Vicki ticked them off with her fingers: "In this relationship there is no alcohol problem; there is better communication"—here she stopped, lifted her shoulders in a shrug, and said, "Pretty much what I wanted in somebody else, it's here. We've pretty much been given it," she said, in a contained tone of voice. I had the impression that while her present situation was clearly much improved, there were reasons she found it less than perfect.

DISRESPECT

Both members of the couple agreed that Christina, now sixteen, had always been an easy, calm, pliable child. "She's passive, like her father," said Vicki in a gratified voice, as if this negative trait had now been transformed into a positive one. Chrissie did her chores at home and was well behaved at school, maintaining high grades and a place on the honor roll.

The partners' five-year-old son, Anthony, was the opposite; he was cut from a different cloth. "He's wild," said Miguel, "as in hitting kids at school. Punching his sister. Tony is very aggressive."

"He's just started kindergarten, so we're trying to wean him out of it," said Vicki. "He's a boy, so he's real physical. Likes to wrestle, but yeah, he is aggressive." She laughed, as if these signs of male aggression didn't really displease her.

"I would have to say the kid is physical a lot," said Miguel, frowning.

"He's just a boy," Vicki defended their son, and she laughed again.

I was silent, but I couldn't help reflecting about the ways in which children absorb the tension in a household and "speak" their feelings through their behavior. Did Tony's hostile attacks on those around him speak of something going on in the household that he was acting out?

As the interview continued, I learned that Miguel and his sister, one year younger, had been raised in a single-parent household. His mother had fled an abusive marriage, and the family had subsisted on state aid and occasional small jobs while Miguel was growing up. For a period of his life—from when he was eight to twelve years old—he had lived with his maternal grandparents in Puerto Rico. As he looked back upon his childhood, he felt that his mother had done "the best she could do to raise us the right way, and I think she did a very good job." At age thirty three, he remained close to her and valued her counsel—which is, by the way, a cultural trait in Puerto Rican families, where motherhood is a highly respected status. "My mom is a neat person. She's very active, energetic. She loves to clean," said Miguel.

"Does she help out at your house?" I asked.

"Yeah, oh yeah, she can't stand still," he said, shifting his body forward on the sofa, as if the very thought of his industrious mom made him want to leap up out of his seat.

There was a pause, during which I looked at each of the partners in turn. Then I asked them both what they considered to be the greatest strength in their relationship. Miguel was the one to answer: "Communication," he said.

Communication was a word that popped up often in this couple's narrative, and I was curious about what it meant to them. "Does 'communicating' mean that you can let each other know about problems, or that you can solve problems together, or what does it mean?" I asked.

"Talking our problems out, and not blowing our rooftops—in other words, not yelling and arguing with each other. That doesn't get anybody anywhere," Miguel stated.

I paused a moment, then asked, "Do you ever do that—blow your rooftops?"

He shrugged. "Yeah, we often argue, but eventually the fight will turn, and we'll talk our way out of it at the end." He glanced at his wife, his expression doubtful, as if he feared she might disapprove of his openness.

She didn't seem troubled. "Who's the person who blows up first?" I asked them both, and Vicki answered swiftly: "It's me. Whatever comes into my mind, I speak out."

"Then would you say that the greatest strength about this relationship is that you can blow up and yet you can get to 'yes' at some point?" I directed this question to Miguel, but it was Vicki who responded again, "Right."

"The major problem in this relationship is . . . what, would you say?" I asked this question of both members of the pair.

"Disrespect," answered Miguel promptly. I jumped slightly at the sound of this word, for I was aware that *respect* is an attribute of supreme importance in the Puerto Rican culture in which he had grown up.

"Disrespect," I repeated, then asked him, "Vicki disrespecting you or you disrespecting Vicki?"

"We both disrespect each other," Miguel replied. "She'll say something nasty about me, and then I'll call her a nasty name she won't like, and we'll get into an argument status. Actually it's a common situation now."

A thought popped into my mind at this moment: it was of their "wild" five-year-old son, who might very well be expressing the confusion of a child whose parents seemed to be getting into an "argument status" very frequently. Was the boy's aggression expressing the turbulent feelings of a child bathed in all this familial tension?

NAME-CALLING

Although they had been quarreling often in the recent past, the names that they flung at each other in the heat of their battles involved no ethnic stereotyping. "The words I don't like, honestly, would be *loser* or *mama's boy*," said Miguel in the course of our conversation about their frequent arguments.

Vicki giggled, embarrassed. "What word would she hate?" I asked him.

"The b-word," he responded, after a brief hesitation.

"*Bitch?*" I asked, and they both laughed and shook their heads. The word in question was *ball-buster*, Miguel told me.

"So the major problem is that when you get into fights, you call each other names that really strike home? That hit below the belt?"

"Yes," both said, almost in unison.

"Or it could be my embarrassing you," said Vicki, turning to her spouse. "You hate it when I do that."

"How does she embarrass you?" I asked him.

He shrugged, then said that they could be in the middle of a conversation in front of friends or family, and Vicki would jump in and start correcting his grammar or the way he was expressing himself. "I'll give her a look, but she doesn't stop. Later on, I tell her, 'Vicki, you shouldn't do that, not in front of other people,' and then we'll get into an argument."

"What's that about?" I asked Vicki.

"Oh, if he's saying something, and I think the word is wrong, or the grammar is wrong, or he said it wrong, then I'll correct him. And it gets him furious; he flips out. He doesn't get it, that I'm only teasing." This kind of barbed teasing, laced with affection, is perfectly acceptable in many Italian families.

I turned to Miguel. "So you don't want to be corrected in public?"

"I don't mind being corrected. It's just the ways she says it, in this snooty tone of voice. And I'll shake my head," he said, shaking his head in the negative to demonstrate. He heard these "helpful corrections" as disrespectful put-downs.

"And you think of the b-word?" I asked him.

He didn't reply. Then he said, "Everybody gets this funny look on their faces when she's putting out this kind of stuff, like I'm kind of ignorant, and——" He pulled up short in midsentence.

"How do you feel about that, Vicki? Do you think he has a point?" I asked.

Vicki, two spots of crimson in her cheeks, said that for her it was all part of just fooling around. "Yeah, we fight, but eventually we calm down and get to a place where we're just joking about it. "Like he'll say, 'What do you want me to do? Get the dictionary out? What's with speaking so precisely?' We end up laughing about it."

Nevertheless, it sounded to me as if this was being experienced as public disrespect by a man whose cultural conditioning would make such incidents seem anything but humorous.

STEPPARENTING

When I asked Miguel what the experience of stepparenting had been like for him, he exhaled deeply and said, "Whew, a lot of work." When I asked him to elaborate upon this statement, however, he fell silent.

"Can you say more about that?" I asked him again.

"Tell her," said Vicki, inclining toward her husband. "Tell her what you tell me all the time, about *your* ways of raising a daughter and my ways!"

"Tell her," repeated Miguel, mumbling under his breath. Then he said, "I'm a little bummed out when it comes to girls. I'm a little strict—I don't know how to put it."

"Go ahead," urged Vicki, leaning even farther in his direction.

There was another long pause, which ended with Miguel saying, "It's hard, I don't know how to put it all together."

"Try," I said, and after another drawn-out, uncomfortable silence, he asked, "What was the question again?"

I laughed, said, "What has the experience of stepfathering been like for you, Miguel?"

"How do you feel about it?" Vicki urged her spouse.

"I guess it's been okay. It's been a learning experience, that's for sure. I mean her daughter is the only female I basically raised." His gaze had shifted to the wall behind me, and it was clear that he was treading water.

"Christina was a four-year-old girl when you and Vicki got together," I said. "And I'm getting the idea, from what you said just now, that it's been hard for you in some ways. In what ways has it been hard?" I pressed him.

"Is it difficult for you to be stepparenting Chrissie?" Vicki echoed my question, addressing Miguel directly. "Because she's not yours."

He shook his head. "It's not that it's so difficult. It's just—I can't share that one," he said. He shook his head again, said he'd "take a pass." The stepparenting question was one he couldn't or wouldn't expand upon.

I turned to Vicki and asked if she could answer for him.

"Yeah, I think so. It was hard for him at first. It's probably still hard for him because I'm a control freak. I want my kid raised *my* way." There was a note of determination in her voice.

What was "her way" and what was "his," I began to ask, but she interrupted. "I have my beliefs, and I know the ways my parents brought me up. I'm not saying the way his mother brought him up—or his sister—was wrong. But the way his mother raised his sister up is the way he wants me to treat my daughter!" A flush of high color suffused her cheeks.

"What way is that?" I asked her.

"His sister never got to go anywhere. Never got to go to a friend's house and sleep over. Never had a group of friends at her own house. She wasn't even allowed to join the Girl Scouts! I know this only because his sister told me herself," Vicki said with disapproval in her voice.

"So your sister had a very strict upbringing," I addressed myself to Miguel. "What was the fear? That she was going to lose her virginity or that something awful would happen to her?"

"Yeah—something like that," he said.

"That's what is in their heads," said Vicki, referring either to her husband's family or to Puerto Rican families in general.

"Right," Miguel agreed. It was clear that their cultural differences were intensifying the typical polarizing issues of a stepparent and a biological parent. Miguel's much more conservative Puerto Rican values were pushing him even further toward a strict authoritarian stance, while Vicki's easygoing ways felt completely beyond dispute to her—and neither one of them seemed to be curious about or interested in trying to understand their differences.

"The friction here is that I'm a bit more free with Chrissie. Not that I would permit anything at all! But him"—she gestured at her husband—"he just doesn't trust people. His way is that you're only safe inside the family. So his sister was always home, always with his mother. That's it, daughter and mother. But the way I was brought up and the way I'm bringing up my daughter is something he doesn't agree with! Chrissie got to do sports and sleepovers; she got very involved in the Girl Scouts. Miguel would like to see her kept homebound, like his sister."

Vicki's tone was defiant. I thought of the fact that she herself was the parent of an out-of-wedlock child and had believed no other man would ever want her for this reason.

Gazing at Miguel, I asked him quietly, "In other words, your family looks on the outside world as dangerous for a female? It scares you as far as a girl is concerned?"

"Yes," he said. I could see that the latitude that his American-ized Italian wife was allowing her daughter was something haz-ardous in the eyes of this traditionally minded Puerto Rican man. I looked from one of them to the other, then asked, "Is this the biggest source of conflict between the two of you?"

"Basically, yes," said Miguel.

"Yes, because that's what's in their heads," repeated Vicki dog-gedly. She and Miguel seemed to be involved in a collision of deeply held beliefs deriving from the cultural schemas they'd assimilated while growing up in their two vastly different social environments.

NOT IN MY HOUSE

In a broader sense, the crisis of Christina's blooming woman-hood was the most problematic of the couple's current concerns. Miguel had intense feelings about the young woman's behavior, but since Vicki was the real parent, he felt powerless to make or enforce any rules.

I asked the partners if they could give me an example of a recent incident regarding the ways this issue played out in their daily lives. "Oh yes," said Vicki easily, explaining that Christina had a romantic attachment, a boy she'd been going out with from the time she was almost fifteen to the present. His name was Juan.

"Just recently, this boyfriend has started coming over, and he"—she pointed to Miguel—"he's had a heart attack. I mean a complete, all-out heart attack! He keeps saying, 'This should not be happening. This boy should not be here!' I say, 'She's sixteen; it has to be happening. I'd rather she moon around here, in my face, than, than do it out in the street by herself.'"

"I don't agree. I don't think this should be happening at all." Miguel's expression was stony.

I asked him what he would like to see happening instead.

"I would like to see her grow up and finish college. Then she could date," he replied.

"At what age?" I asked, and he shrugged, said, "Not at sixteen. I would say at least eighteen or nineteen. I don't like the smooching, the hugging, the kissing. Not in my face. Not in *my* house," said Miguel, sounding indignant.

Vicki said she agreed with him on that point and that she'd told Chrissie that she didn't want to see her and Juan hanging all over each other. "I told her I don't want to *see* it," she repeated, forcefully.

"To me, that's total disrespect!" put in Miguel heatedly. "The boy should know that when you're in somebody's home—and the parents are there—you should know better than to put your hands all over her."

Vicki told me hastily that they weren't going into each other's shirts or anything like that. "I'm not saying they're doing anything wrong," Miguel conceded. Vicki's agreement seemed to have calmed him down.

I asked him if he'd prefer it if Chrissie's boyfriend never came to their house at all.

"No, no." Miguel retreated further. "He's a good kid, and I respect that sooner or later she's going to have somebody she wants to go out with. But at age sixteen, it's just too early. I don't accept that." His expression had hardened once again.

Vicki said that Miguel kept saying that he knows what *he* did with girls when he was sixteen. "He tells Chrissie, 'There you go, you'll be in trouble before you know it.'"

"What does she say to that?" I asked.

"She says to him, 'Well, I'm not like that; I'm not going to let that happen!' And I tell him, 'You have to trust me that I raised her properly to know better.' He tells me, 'When she comes home pregnant, I don't want to hear any complaints coming from you!' And I say that she is never going to come home pregnant. I've put enough training in her, she knows right from wrong!"

"What you're saying is that you raised her in a way that makes you feel you can trust her to take care of herself?" I asked Vicki.

"Correct," she answered proudly. She sat up ramrod straight in her seat. Miguel was glowering. He, as stepparent, had moved into the firmer, harsher, authoritarian (not authoritative) position, even though he could not enforce his rules. His approach was in opposition to Vicki's more easygoing, trusting, loving, (overly?) permissive role, and I wondered whether she herself, as an unwed mother, was aware of the model she had presented to her daughter. As most therapists will attest, it is well known that the curious ways in which certain familial "mistakes" are repeated from generation to generation count among the more riveting statistics available.

GOSSIP

As our interview was drawing to a close, I asked Vicki if there were things that she would like to talk about with Miguel but that never did get talked about. The idea seemed to strike her as funny, and she laughed. "No, I have a big mouth! I always talk to him. Whenever I want to say something, I say it."

I turned to Miguel. "How about you? Are there issues you would like to talk about more with Vicki? Things that you don't talk about?" When he didn't reply, I said, "You're looking very thoughtful."

He cleared his throat. "I would like to say—yes—about the gossip."

Vicki turned in her seat. "You want to talk to me more about *that*?" she asked.

"Yeah, you know I hate that. People gossiping about our relationship—and things." He looked at her apprehensively, as if fearing that he'd already said too much.

"What kind of gossip?" I asked.

"It seems to me that a lot of people make a lot of assumptions about our relationship. They try to put their two cents in, and it's something I really don't . . ." Again, his sentence trailed off. I told him I was unclear about what he meant and asked him to give me an example.

Miguel lowered his head, muttered that there were too many people talking about the way he and Vicki were with each other. "We do disrespect each other," he said, speaking to his lap.

"Which people are these? Friends?" I asked.

Looking up at me, then over at Vicki, he said, "Friends, my family, her family, whoever. That's one of the things I can't stand."

"What do you think they're saying?" I inquired.

He stared at me a moment, inhaled, and then let out a deep breath. "Things about the way I am. I *do* have a temper, and I know I say things to her that I shouldn't say. And I know she goes back and talks to people. I don't know who they are."

"My sisters or my friends," said Vicki immediately.

"Then they give her advice, like tell her to come back home and tell me off. Stuff like that, and then she comes back at me with a lot of spite and resentment. From then on we're into a big grudge battle, and everyone's there on the sidelines heckling us on." He was keeping his eyes firmly fixed upon mine, and avoiding his wife's wide-eyed stare.

"What you're saying is that whatever conflict is in your relationship with Vicki you would like to keep just between the two of you?" I paraphrased his statement back to him, and he met my eye and nodded gratefully. What came to my mind at that moment was a half-joking remark an Italian friend had once made to me: "Whenever anyone in my entire family system has a headache, the rest of us all take an aspirin." Discussing her issues with her sisters and her friends came naturally to Vicki, given her background. But these discussions were highly disturbing to her husband and clearly didn't help Vicki calm down and become more constructive. Quite the contrary, they intensified the couple's difficulties.

Not only were she and Miguel dealing with the parenting and insider/outsider challenges posed by their union, they were still working within two very different cultural frameworks that stood in need of an empathetic translator.

Toward the end of the interview, I paused and gave each of them a long look. "Has this remarriage been a success, would you say?" I asked, my voice thoughtful.

Before replying, they sat there for a moment, both staring at me fixedly. "Yeah, it has, it definitely has," said Miguel at last. "We have our ups and downs, but that's the way we are. We have our ups and downs. But successful? For sure." He turned and gave his wife a long, adoring look.

"He sure doesn't give up," said Vicki, gratified. "Because every time I get really pissed at him and want to kick him out, he says, 'I'm not leaving. We're going to work this out. I'm not leaving.'"

"Never," said Miguel feelingly.

The tensions between this pair seemed to blow up and then calm down as if, at some level, they didn't take these emotional dramas very seriously. Still, I wondered what effect all these "ups and downs" were going to have on their developing children, for it is well established that growing children are highly sensitive to parental fighting. All in all, it seemed clear to me that this tempestuous marriage would endure, but I wondered if these partners would ever stop disputing about whose cultural rules were the "right" ones and learn to tolerate—and even respect—the inevitable differences between them.

CHAPTER NINE

A Charmed Life:
Margaret and Bruce Gray,
2011

Margaret Gray had told me on the telephone that she and her husband worked together as venture capitalists and philanthropists. "We've not only started business projects that prosper, but we also give away a lot of money," she had said. Then she'd added, sounding almost defensive, that their philanthropic activities actually took up a good deal of time and thought.

I had the distinct impression that Margaret had grown up in privileged circumstances, for she spoke with an air of command and entitlement.

Still, I was unprepared for the grandeur of the Grays' large, white clapboard home, situated on a wooded waterfront site in Darien, Connecticut. The couple led me through a large foyer and living room and into a sun-drenched den. We settled ourselves in this comfortable room, which was graced with oversized windows that afforded a dramatic view of the Long Island Sound. I embarked upon the interview by asking the partners their current ages and how long they had been together.

It was Bruce who responded. He was fifty-eight and Margaret was fifty-four. They had been married for nineteen years, and this was a second marriage, following upon divorce, for both of them. I turned to Margaret and asked about her first marriage. How long had it lasted, and what had it been like? Had she had children? What had brought about that marriage's ending?

To my surprise, it was Bruce who answered again. Margaret had been married for six years, he said. At the time of their own marriage, she'd had a three-year-old son, Charlie, and a five-year-old daughter, Trisha. I made a few notes and then looked up to meet his wife's steady, green-eyed gaze. Margaret Gray is a tall woman with auburn hair, which she wore upswept into a tidy, thick chignon. She was wearing a black sweater, tan trousers, and no makeup or jewelry.

"Margaret," I asked her directly, "tell me a bit about your first marriage, and what led to the breakup."

Margaret cocked her head to one side, reflected for a few moments, and then said that her first husband, Alan, was a person who was completely self-contained. He did what he wanted to do, no matter where, when, or what the circumstances. "For instance, we might be sitting down to a meal with my family, and my dad would be taking orders for the barbecue, and we're all getting ready to enjoy a dinner together. That could well be the moment that Alan would say, 'I'm going to go for a run.' Then off he'd go, and my father would try to hold the steaks. Alan was always very nice about it, and, he'd say, 'It doesn't matter if you guys go ahead without me, and I'll just slide in when I return.'" Her face clouded over, "Well, *no.* This is a family activity," she said in an anger-tinged voice.

"It isn't that Alan lacks a good heart," she added more pacifically. "He has one. If you were stranded by the side of the road, he would stop. But he is a social clod."

"In other words, he doesn't care about other people?" I asked.

"He doesn't connect," Margaret replied.

"As I see it from an outsider's perspective," put in Bruce, "he's an absentee because he doesn't know *how* to connect. He's into role-playing the father and the husband, but he wants the appearance, not the reality."

Margaret nodded her agreement. "He wanted the picture of the family on the Christmas card, but he didn't want the family's mess. He often traveled." She shrugged. Clearly, her ex-spouse's absence was a boon for this happy pair, but I wondered what it meant to her children. How had they, especially five-year-old Trisha, actually experienced their real father's decampment? Young children have no language for their losses.

"On the other hand," Bruce continued, "Alan had no idea of how offensive his behavior could be to other people, to observers. When we first met I was an outsider—just a friend of Margaret's brother— and I was shocked by how insulting and demeaning he was to her. In front of everyone! I mean, she was his wife, and the mother of his two kids; I found his behavior amazing. It was so sexist, like something out of the fifties."

TWO SETS OF PARENTS

Although both Bruce and Margaret came from wealthy business backgrounds, their early family lives had been very different. "With your parents, there was this real passion," said Margaret, turning to Bruce.

"My parents were best friends," Bruce informed me.

"Their relationship was at the center," said Margaret.

"Yes, and she doesn't like me to say so," he gestured with his head toward his wife, "but as parents, they were selfish. It was all about them. They went out to dinner five times a week; we rarely ate together. I mean to say that they were supportive but not particularly attentive. They never came down to kid level, never connected as friends.

"I, on the other hand, am absolutely, positively friendly with my kids. There is no question: my best friends aside from Margaret *are* our children. I want to know what they are thinking. I respect what they are thinking. I know they're not as widely experienced as I am, but from early on, we've had a connection that I never had as a kid. I was disciplined constantly. I was rebelling constantly from the time I was about seven."

The son and daughter born to Margaret's first marriage were now in their early twenties. The Grays had had two children together, both daughters. Evie and Margo were now in their teens. When their combined family was growing up, stated Bruce, they'd all eaten together seven times a week, not just two or three. He was as passionate about parenting as his parents had been about one another.

Margaret's parents had been a misalliance and had later divorced, so she was loath to judge Bruce's in-love parents equally harshly. "His folks had some real solidness and goodness," she said, "but ironically, my own folks' problems made my dad want to be with us kids more. I mean, he was there because we were there, so he was happy to connect with us. I didn't fully realize that until I was in my forties, but that makes for a very different sibling dynamic. We felt as if we were on a sinking ship, where we might be abandoned, so we bonded very closely as children. Bruce's siblings were jockeying to get more parental sun, but there was never enough sunshine for everyone. So they weren't connected to one another as siblings."

"There was not enough sustenance for everyone," I paraphrased her remark, and she nodded, smiled, and said, "Because the gods were up on Mt. Olympus doing their thing."

IN GUILT LAND

Bruce's first marriage had lasted five years, in the legal sense. But he had been separated from his first wife, Rosemary, for three of those years and simply not gotten around to obtaining a divorce.

"Rosemary and I met in my second year of law school. She came from a strict Catholic family, and when we moved in together, her dad essentially disowned her. I felt responsible for her, and I paid for her to finish college. The two of us got along famously until she started becoming intensely jealous and intolerant of relationships I'd had before I ever met her. She was so resentful and threatened by anything from my past—it had me walking on pins and needles. I felt so guilty all the time, even though I wasn't doing anything to merit it! Just before we were married, an ex-girlfriend from high school came to visit me. I didn't see a problem, but Rosemary was deeply hurt and shaken by that absolutely innocent event. She never let me forget it."

Bruce shrugged his shoulders, ran a hand across his forehead as if trying to wipe out a painful memory. "Anyhow, we got married because we were in too deep, and I thought we should. I thought I'd made a commitment. But after the wedding, life went on the same way. Rosemary was such a jealous and demanding person that I was living in a kind of guilt land. Then out of the blue, about two years into the marriage, she announced that she wanted a divorce. I was stunned, shattered. But as time passed, I thought, 'This is the best thing ever.'

"A few months later, Rosemary came back and proposed a reconciliation." Bruce laughed, said, "For me, it was like—are you kidding? The split-up really broke my heart, but the marriage was never right. I gave her everything we had when we broke up, but for me, it was over. We'd gotten married on the basis of a relationship we'd had much earlier, but it wasn't the one we had at the time."

The pair had had no children. "You were lucky about that," I commented.

"Yes, very lucky," he said. He sighed, added with a half smile, "We did have a great dog, though, and she got him. But seriously, she was critical, demanding, and unsupportive from the outset of the marriage. We were not on the same page at all."

I asked him to define the major difference between this current relationship and that failed one. Bruce drew in a deep breath, then exhaled deeply. "Everything," he said. "Margaret and I are totally honest and spontaneous. We don't put up any fronts. There are no demands laid down, ever, in the sense of 'you can't do this' or 'you must do that.' There is an 'I would appreciate it if you would do this, please,' or 'I can't stand it when you do that kind of stuff,' but there is total honesty between us. Happily, I have no reason to resort to any subterfuge; there is complete transparency between us."

"No guilt?" I asked.

"No guilt for any reason," he said, shaking his head. "I buy into that Mark Twain comment that you should never do anything so bad that you have to lie about it."

"So then, no jealousy here?" I asked, looking from one member of the couple to the other.

"No jealousy," said Bruce. "Margaret knows I have absolute love for her."

SURPRISES

When I asked the Grays to name the biggest surprise that this second marriage had brought to each of them, Margaret was quick to reply: she had been surprised by his good manners. "Being a good roommate goes a long way," she said, "and Bruce is such a considerate person. If he's going downstairs, he will stop and ask, 'Would you like me to get you something?' If he is passing by the store, he'll call and ask if there's anything I need. We'd never lived together before we were married, because I didn't want to put my children into any kind of testing situation. So what surprised me was how much difference this kind of thoughtfulness makes."

I turned to Bruce, who simply shrugged his shoulders as if

to say he didn't have any ready answer. Margaret then said that another thing that had surprised her was the realization that while they were having long, intimate telephone conversations in the period before their marriage, Bruce had also been watching a basketball or baseball game. "He was multitasking," she said ruefully.

"I was rarely multitasking," protested Bruce. "I really wasn't."

"I had no idea how much television he needs to watch in a day," continued Margaret. I knew how great the intimacy and the sex would be, so the TV was probably my biggest surprise."

I asked Bruce how much TV he watched in a typical day. He said he watched all of the political programs, left leaning and right leaning, from the late afternoon until about eleven p.m. "I also read a lot about politics. I'm very absorbed in events as they're unfolding." He added that he also liked sports events, and the kids enjoyed watching them with him.

Margaret said irritably that the news programs repeated themselves over and over again, so that there was this constant racket in the background. "There are always guests who are fighting, and the news is being turned into a horse race. At the same time, there are lots of important news stories that are being left out, simply ignored."

I sought Bruce's gaze and asked whether this was a problem for the pair of them. "I don't have a big problem," he answered, his voice bland.

"But if this is a problem for Margaret?"

There was a silence, and then Margaret said, "This is something we haven't really worked out. The world wouldn't blow up if we didn't watch the news tonight, and we did something else. If we read a book or watched a movie—just anything different."

My thought was that if one member of a couple was having a problem, there was an unresolved problem in the pair's relationship. But as an interviewer I was there to listen, not offer unsolicited advice. There was another brief silence, and I decided to move along.

I looked at Bruce and repeated my question about the biggest surprise this remarriage had held for him. He said that for him, there had been no big surprises. "We had been friends for a long time before we got into a dating relationship. She was married, so we just had a friendship—and that friendship got closer and closer over time. We had some of the funniest experiences of my life, laughing and laughing together. It got to a point where we were just so connected that a single eye contact or a hand squeeze conveyed a whole lot of information.

"At the time when we got married it was by far the best relationship I'd ever had in my life, but it wasn't nearly as deep as it later became. So if you ask me if I was surprised that it got even better and more remarkable as I parented her kids—and we had two of our own—the answer is no. Was it new? Yes, it was real new. All of it was new," he concluded happily.

"It's a lovely story," I said, moved by his intensity. I turned to Margaret, who was nodding her agreement, her cheeks pink with pleasure. A moment later, though, she leaned forward to touch her husband's knee and to ask him if he hadn't actually been surprised by some of the issues that came up around stepparenting. He looked startled, and for a moment, time seemed to stop.

"We'll be coming to that," I assured her.

BIG BLUNDERS

Because Margaret was the sole member of the couple who had brought children to the marriage, I turned to Bruce and said, "I guess you are the only stepparent here, so can you tell me what the experience has been like for you?"

Bruce reflected for a few moments before responding. "In many ways, I've been fortunate as a stepdad, because when we married the kids were so young—three and five years old. Also, they knew we were getting married for many months beforehand . . ." He left his sentence unfinished, then said, "I just loved those kids to death. I adored them from early on. They were so little; Charlie was still a toddler, and I'd met him when he was in diapers. At first, Trisha was the more openly affectionate, and it's hard not to fall in love with a little girl when she is so attached to you. She was always jumping in my lap, always all over me. And it was like that until she was eleven."

For some reason Bruce sighed, then said in a more subdued tone of voice, "But I was also at an advantage because their father was so distant. Geographically, I mean, because he was on the other side of the world for most of their lives."

"Where was he?" I asked them.

"Traveling in Asia, for the most part," said Margaret. "He was far away."

"We would see him a couple of times a year," put in Bruce, "and from my own point of view, that was ideal. It was perfect."

This statement gave me pause, for while many adults think they can exile absent parents into a forgotten past, stepchildren often feel as if they have a hole in their heart where the "real" dad or mom ought to be. This sense of loss and possibly a loyalty bind ("If I love my stepparent, will I lose whatever shreds of my true father remain to me?") frequently lies dormant until the stepchild reaches adolescence, a phenomenon known as the "sleeper effect." Then, as research studies have shown, previously well-adjusted stepchildren often experience a huge upsurge of conflicted, upsetting feelings.

The abrupt awakening of these feelings of loss and divided loyalties is probably due to cognitive, intellectual, and hormonal changes, as well as to the developmental challenge of the adolescent years—that of forging an authentic identity. As a result, however, the stepchild may become a rebel without an obvious cause: volatile, rebellious, and angrily rejecting of his or her loving, caring stepparent.

"Alan didn't try to torpedo us or to torpedo me with the children." Bruce's voice had grown thoughtful. "He did try to pee on the bushes a bit and establish his territory; but he was utterly unsuccessful until our oldest, Trisha, was in her teenage years. I made a bad mistake then, and it fed into his line." His head had dropped, and he was speaking into his chest as if embarrassed.

When I asked him to tell me about the mistake, he looked up and met my eye. "I spanked her once. It was at a time when she was just going on twelve, and she was being so rude and obnoxious to everyone. But I should never have done that. There was tension between us for years."

"What was the incident that caused you to spank her?" I kept my voice neutral, though I was taken aback by this revelation. His behavior—spanking a preteen girl—had been completely out of bounds, and it was somehow even more so given that she was not his biological daughter. I wondered what had triggered this man, whose wife so valued his manners and thoughtfulness, into so uncharacteristic an act. "Was Margaret around?" I asked him.

Bruce ran a quick hand over his close-cropped, dark hair and told me that she had been at home, but not nearby when that event occurred. He went on to say that he and Trish had actually had a couple of hurtful clashes during the period before the spanking occurred. "Up until that time we'd been very close in every respect. But all of a sudden, she began using such foul language, being nasty to adults, slamming doors—she even slammed her bedroom door in my face as I stood there! It was as if one day she'd been my loving daughter, and the next day I was lower than dirt."

He sighed. "I realize now that this behavior was no different from that of any other twelve-year-old girl. You've got to respect their space, and so on," he said uncertainly. "But I embarrassed her badly in front of our longtime housekeeper, whose opinion she values greatly. I told her she was being rude and disrespectful to Maureen, and she said she was not, and I said she was. I then marched her down the hall to Maureen and asked, 'Am I right or wrong? Is she rude to you?' I can't remember how the conversation went, but the housekeeper said that it was true; she was being insolent to her all the time.

"That was terribly upsetting for Trisha—and in retrospect, it should have just as upsetting for me. I should *never* have put the kid in that position; she felt completely humiliated. But she did have such a noxious mouth. She was a twelve-year-old, but she was way out of control. So I spanked her. Not severely. But what really freaked her out was that I took her over my knees and gave her one whack on the behind. In other words, I took control, I just dominated her."

"You dominated her verbally too," said Margaret. She turned to me and said, "Bruce would have made the most amazing court-room litigator."

Without responding directly to his wife's remark, Bruce said to me, "Trisha and I were clashing a lot at that time, but I believe that if it hadn't been for those two events—embarrassing her to the extreme and proving her wrong, and immobilizing her and whacking her on the behind—we might have gone on clashing intellectually and philosophically on different topics but stayed as closely connected as we had always been." He sounded mournful and regretful, as if he wished he could undo those two episodes and return to a happier period in their relationship.

Bruce cleared his throat and went on to say that he'd had his tussles and difficulties with his younger stepchild, Charlie, but the two of them had enjoyed a close relationship always. "I do have a dominant vocal presence," admitted Bruce, but let this pass with a shrug of his shoulders. "I think that because Trisha was older when we got married and because of that bad inter-action, we got to the point where she actually screamed at me, 'You are not my father!'" As he repeated these repudiating words, Bruce looked stricken.

"Those famous, awful words," I commented sympathetically.

"It was so painful," he said in a low, almost inaudible voice.

I thought of the disjunction between the abundant research

on remarriage and the fact that so little of that information is made available to remarried people. If it had been, Bruce and Margaret might have been forewarned about the importance of children's losses and loyalty binds—even when an ex-spouse is off the scene—and how frequently these issues come home to roost during the period of the stepchild's adolescence. Then one or both of them could have sat down with Trisha and helped her talk these feelings out. The Grays could even have taken a pointer or two from "Patricia's script" (see chapter 2) and helped this beloved daughter understand that there was room in her heart to love *both* her stepfather and her real father as well—that the two relationships need not compete for the only place in her heart that existed.

"Trish and I were at odds for several years after that," Bruce said sadly. "Trisha was very hurt, but I believe she always loved me. She just didn't like me so much for a while," he added with a self-conscious little laugh.

Margaret, looking concerned, put in soothingly, "Remember, though, the many times she would let her guard down—how grateful she was when you helped her build the aqueduct for her high school Roman project."

Bruce then recalled a time when Trisha, at age fourteen, had gotten very drunk at a pajama party given by one of her girl-friends. She had begun vomiting uncontrollably, in such a frightening way that her girlfriend's mother, a nurse, had called 911. Margaret had been out of town, and Bruce had rushed to the friend's house in time to accompany Trisha in the ambulance that sped them to the hospital. "I walked her through the whole experience—the doctors, the social workers. And while she was completely inebriated, she kept saying, 'I love you, Bruce. I love you, Bruce.'" This rapprochement had, however, not lasted. "My guess is that this was because I hadn't really grasped the depth of the feelings Trisha was struggling with. Also, I didn't have a clue about how to go about repairing the relationship."

Margaret now commented, her voice careful, that they had a number of remarried friends with whom they socialized. "Most stepparents tell me that there is always some quantifiable difference between their feelings for their own biological children and their stepchildren," she said.

Bruce disagreed immediately. He said, in a voice charged with emotion, that his feelings for his two stepkids and for their mutual children were much the same. He loved them all very, very deeply.

"Of course, it is more difficult with Trisha, who came into my life when she was five," he conceded. "But Charlie is my kid. We make good eye contact and we understand each other. We have similar views about many things. With Trisha—well, there was a time after that spanking event when she wouldn't even look at me." He had a catch in his voice. It was evident that he still suffered intense regret about the bad interactions that had occurred so many years earlier.

Out of the blue, he added, "To be honest, I'm jealous of Margaret's relationship with Trisha." Margaret looked at him, shook her head as if to dismiss this silly idea. She told me that her oldest daughter was now a graduate student at Princeton, and she called home constantly. It was worrisome; it was too much. She thought that Trish was overconnected. "It's not healthy," she said. I was silent, though I believe that the myth that young adults don't need their parents is just that—a myth. Or perhaps Margaret's remark was simply meant to be consoling.

"Nevertheless, I'm jealous because they talk every day," Bruce said. He was the stuck outsider in this relationship that was so important to him.

"It's not me calling her," said Margaret defensively. "It's her calling me." She was the stuck insider, and it hurt her to be hurting him.

"I'm still jealous," he repeated, "because you two talk every day. Sometimes twice a day."

"Why does that make you jealous?" I asked him quietly.

"Because *I* want to talk to her," he replied. "And if I answer the phone, she asks for her mom. So I say, 'And how are you?' And she says, 'I'm fine, but can I talk to Mom?' He looked despondent. "It's hard not to feel underappreciated when you're being ignored." Then he added, as though to comfort himself, "Of course, there was a period of time when it was way, way worse."

Margaret laid a gentle hand on his thigh and said, "I know, Bruce. It's hard."

MONEY, SEX, AND TEAMWORK

I asked the Grays how they managed money, how they made financial decisions, and whether money ever tended to be a source of tension between the pair of them. They hesitated, looked at one another in puzzlement, almost as though I had asked a question in a foreign language.

I explained that remarried couples handled their funds in a variety of ways: some keep their accounts completely separate (the two-pot family). Some keep their accounts separate but have a third fund, which is used for ongoing household expenditures (the three-pot family). Some simply pool their resources (the one-pot family). "Do you have a pooled account?" I asked them.

"The answer is yes," said Margaret. "I couldn't do that when I was married to Alan. Even though we were both from comfortable families and he earned a good living, he would look at the checkbook and say, 'You spent *what* for a dress?' In that marriage, I absolutely had to have my own credit cards, because he was on my neck about every single purchase. For years I kept a separate checking account because I had been so beaten up by him. He was very controlling, very tight. And Bruce is really much better at numbers. He's the one who'll ask, 'Why is the water bill three times higher than it was? There must be a leak somewhere that needs to be fixed.' Bruce was the better person to keep the checkbook, and so over time I was able to say, 'Okay, he's not going to yell at me about decisions I make.' We're involved in lots of stuff together, and we are both signing checks. But he looks over the accounts, and he's the one managing the money—which is the best division of labor."

"Do you ever quarrel about money?"

They both shook their heads and said no. "It is never an issue," Bruce appended.

"It's not that it *couldn't* be an issue," said Margaret. "I grew up in a family with lots of money, and believe me, you can really fight about money, no matter how much you have."

"Before you married, did you look into each other's books or do any kind of prenup?" I looked at Margaret. "Did you think about the division of inheritances among four kids?"

Margaret replied that there was enough money for all four of her children. "They got cut out of my first husband's father's will totally, but it doesn't matter. Because they are our heirs, and they will get enough from us."

Bruce added that several years ago he had approached his father and said, "I hope you live forever, but if you don't, leave your money to my siblings. Margaret and I are well fixed." He and Margaret were so secure that he had removed his family from his dad's will voluntarily.

I smiled, said that money was clearly not an issue. Then I asked them, "The greatest strength about this relationship is . . . what?"

Bruce said simply, "We are best friends and we enjoy ourselves together."

"Margaret?" I said, turning to her for her answer.

"Honestly, I think the greatest thing about us is that we have a similar sense of humor. We can laugh at ourselves and at the world, and we are a real team in that way. Nothing upsets me more than when I think we are *not* being a team, and I think that's true for Bruce as well. At the same time, we know what things to take seriously and really care about, and what things to let be. I think we are similar in that way."

Looking from one of them to the other, I said, "It sounds as if you have a good time."

"Yes," said Margaret, echoed by Bruce's "Definitely."

Margaret then told a story about how, shortly after Bruce's mother's death, they had decided to go to Jamaica together to shake off a case of mutual blues. A friend of hers was surprised that they were going by themselves, with no other couples along. She had asked Margaret, "Are you going to have enough to talk about?"

"Now, that thought would never occur to me," said Margaret. "I wouldn't marry somebody I couldn't talk to. I feel sorry for people who have that kind of worry. But you do see them sitting opposite each other in hotels, having breakfast and not saying a word. And it's not a companionable silence. I can be reading, and Bruce is doing something else, and I look up and say, 'Can you believe what I just read in the newspaper?' We are always interacting and connecting with each other, while those couples seem to be moving in parallel lines."

I then asked what was, in their opinion, the major problem in this relationship.

"Fox News," said Bruce immediately, and the three of us laughed. But as I saw it, the lack of reasonable compromise about how they were spending their evenings was a real difficulty they were going to have to resolve. I hesitated, wondering whether to revisit a stepissue, such as their insider/outsider status in regard to Trisha. I even considered asking them if they had ever sat down with the children and talked with them about what it felt like to have an absent dad. But that would have been an overreach, and at that moment I saw Margaret steal a surreptitious glance at her watch. I looked at my own watch; I had been talking with the Grays for about an hour and a half. An early January sunset was transforming a formerly cloudless blue sky into a vista of streaked colors, orange most of all.

"Finally—and this is my last question—what do you think are the major sexual issues that emerge at this time of life?"

Bruce said straightforwardly, "Less frequency because of age."

I turned to Margaret, asked, "What do you see as the major sexual issue?"

"Less frequency because of age."

I looked from one member of the pair to the other. "Does someone want more frequency?"

"Yes. She does," Bruce replied.

"She does," I repeated his statement, meeting Margaret's gaze. She raised an eyebrow, said yes.

"Sure she does," said Bruce, "but I'm not as . . ." He halted in midstatement and then resumed. "When we do have sex, it's always good. There aren't any problems. It works out the right way."

"I think he's more interested in Sean Hannity and Bill O'Reilly," observed Margaret drily. "And also the kids are at an age where they come into our bedroom. They're in there all the time."

Bruce agreed. He said, "It's a combination of that and of aging. Still, I haven't had to turn to Viagra," he added, as if in his defense. He went on to say that there was such a thing as a meaningful encounter. "There is sex, and there is making love with Margaret. And she is the person I've connected with more than anyone else I've ever known. The absolute trust we share. As I get older I'm obviously not as sexually active as I would like to be, but we do have a wonderful relationship—one that's better than anything I've ever known."

Margaret said nothing aloud, but as she looked at him, her expression was tender and affectionate.

"We are charmed; we have a charmed life," continued Bruce. "Not only do we have four basically happy, healthy children and a relatively happy broader family, but we have opportunities to do things together—via our philanthropies, for instance—that are really remarkable. So we flourish and we enjoy ourselves because our strengths are different and we balance each other out in a natural sort of way."

Yes, I thought, even though Bruce had been triggered into behaving badly on that one much-regretted occasion, and even though he was dealing with the decline in sexual appetite that can accompany aging, I could readily agree with his assessment. In this second marriage, Bruce and Margaret Gray had formed a tight and satisfying bond and were indeed living a charmed life.

Epilogue

Over the course of the 1960s, 1970s, and 1980s, "development of the true self" became an idealized personal task, one that took clear precedence over prior commitments—such as those owed to one's mate and one's children. During this period of social upheaval, the divorce rate doubled and then trebled, so I suppose it was inevitable that my husband and I came to number more and more remarried couples among our friends and acquaintances. However, this far more frequent exposure to the phenomenon of remarriage never altered my somewhat romantic view of the institution. I saw remarriage as a spanking new start with a freshly cleaned slate—a second chance at happiness with a newer, more wisely selected spouse/parent handily replacing the original, perhaps imprudently chosen partner. Certainly, I didn't see anything special or different about these couples and their families.

Were these remarried mates happy? I couldn't know. People are very protective of their marriages, and the second (or third) time around, they are even more sensitive to whether their relationships are seen as successful. From my own very casual knowledge of these couples, most appeared to be doing well. True, once in a while someone talked with me about a tricky marital issue. For example, a good friend of mine, the mother of two school-age children, had entered into a second marriage with a well-known journalist who was the father of two teenagers living with his ex-wife. After a few years my friend sorely wanted her new husband to formally adopt her children, but he simply wouldn't hear of it. Apparently he did not wish to share his own biological children's last name with the children of his wife's former marriage. This issue became an ongoing, bitter debate between the members of the pair, and eventually they separated after a decade together.

Another example of a remarriage-linked difficulty was confided to me at a professional luncheon by a perfect stranger who happened to be sitting on my right. This woman told me that although she had no children of her own, she was married to a man who was the parent of three: a daughter, six, and two sons, ages eight and ten. She said she tried to be understanding about how much he missed his kids, but nevertheless took exception to the fact that every evening, her husband spent long periods of time talking to each of them on the phone about their day at school. Then, following those conversations, he would often engage in a friendly wrap-up discussion with his ex-wife about how their mutual children were getting along. While all of this was transpiring, she herself would stretch out on the sofa with a glass of wine and read or watch a TV film alone.

As I now recognize (but surely didn't at that time), at least two major unaddressed remarriage challenges were at play in this couple's relationship. One was the powerful impact of insider/outsider forces: this second wife seemed to become an outsider almost every evening while the first-marriage family's agenda dominated the scene. The second unmet challenge was that of creating a clear boundary around the new couple—albeit a boundary with a hole in it to allow access to the other biological parent. Clearly, in this instance, there was no Dutch door of the kind that Papernow suggests, a door whose top half remains open to facilitate parental discussions of the children's issues and schedules, yet whose bottom half closes firmly to create a barrier between the new and the former marriage in regard to friendly evening chats and inappropriate personal time.

*   *   *

What seems most peculiar to me now, from the vantage point of hindsight, is that I heard these confidences as ordinary marital problems rather than as problematic structural issues endemic to the remarried state itself. It was only during the series of in-depth interviews that I carried out in the late 1990s that I came to realize that the uniting of different biologically related families creates a number of unforeseen difficulties—and that these could not be understood within the framework of a traditional, first-marriage-family model. During that initial effort, one omnipresent problem surely did become very clear to me, and that was the swift emergence of insider/outsider issues in remarried households.

I can readily recall one set of interviews where the wife (the divorced parent of a ten-year-old boy) described the impact of moving into the home of her new husband, a widower with three adolescent sons, ages thirteen, fifteen, and eighteen, the oldest of whom was in college. Shortly after their "beautiful wedding," she said wryly "I instantly became the only female living in an all-male fraternity house."

Before her remarriage, this woman, a high school teacher, had maintained an orderly household. Her own son was a quiet, studious, well-behaved youngster who'd always done his chores quite willingly. But her new spouse's motherless household was being run in a supremely casual style, as it had been ever since his wife's death from cancer some four years earlier.

While she did acknowledge that her stepsons were good-natured young men, their ways of living were unbelievably slovenly. The dishes were never washed until they were stacked up so high that the sink could no longer hold them, and the towels and sheets were filthy. This never seemed to bother their father at all. Still, she had presumed that when she and her son moved into her bridegroom's home, the situation would change. Her expectation had been that this group of hapless males would be *grateful* to her for helping them to get their domestic scene under control. She had entered the household planning to get the place cleaned up, put well-cooked meals on the table, do the laundry, and so on—and to carry out these chores willingly, with everyone pitching in to some minimal degree.

However, in the laid-back, locker-room style of living that prevailed in her new spouse's home, such activities were seen as offensively out of line. Who was this Johnny-come-lately "parent" telling them to straighten up their rooms and make their beds before leaving for school? And what right did she have to initiate these changes in the ways things had always happened—had been happening ever since their mother's death—within the insiders' own, familiar environment? Having survived the painful loss of their "real parent," these boys were grimly set on preventing any further changes—especially changes initiated by this stranger/stepparent—from taking place and disrupting the rhythms of their lives once again.

As my interviews continued, this underlying theme was to be repeated ad infinitum. No matter how wildly different the circumstances might seem to be at an overt, superficial level, often the members of the couple were having these vastly different experiences of the marriage. The outsider was feeling like a displaced person without any voice, while the weary insider was trying to negotiate between honoring the new beloved's needs and convincing the youngsters that nothing fundamental would really change and he or she would always be there for them.

My initial plan had, of course, been to describe the stages of the stepfamily journey as the new couple and their families came together, confronted successive roadblocks, and eventually arrived at a newly integrated family system that included all members of the group. But my conversations with remarried pairs had turned up nothing as tidy as the outline I'd begun with. To be sure, I quickly recognized various phenomena that seemed particular to remarried households, such as insider/outsider difficulties, but they didn't add up to a coherent narrative.

I went so far as to sign up at a local family therapy training institute specifically so I could take a course in stepfamily dynamics. But as it turned out, there was no such course being offered then (and there are still very few available anywhere despite the huge rise in the rates of divorce and remarriage). I *did* have a happy surprise when my name was called out in the student roll call. The whole class burst out into applause because my books were being used in that school as texts in a number of their courses!

Inevitably, as I mention in the Prologue, the result of my initial research on remarriage was that I had to pack up my notes, papers, and tape recordings in a brown carton and store it in the back of a closet. I wasn't sure that box would ever be opened again.

But then, in late 2008, I came across Patricia Papernow's new architectural model, and my aha! moment arrived. This remarkably astute theory lays out the five major challenges of remarriage in a succinct, comprehensible fashion. And not only does this excellent model reduce a great deal of confusion to a manageable discussion, it offers a series of ingenious strategies for working on and building a nourishing, benignly inclusive remarried life.

At present, having researched and thought about the subject of remarriage for more than a decade, I find that what remains most memorable are my conversations with the many couples I interviewed. Each member of the pair always had a different tale to tell, and not infrequently someone expressed himself or herself in ways that verged on the poetic. I saw up close how unmoored the partners often felt as they faced their daily struggles without really understanding that the underlying design of remarriage is different from that of a first-family model. It is immensely difficult to wrap one's head around this fundamental truth.

It is my sincere hope that the stories in this book and the architectural model I found so useful in understanding how remarried relationships unfold—and succeed or are torn asunder—will prove helpful to the many individuals and couples who are undoubtedly coping with similar sorts of difficulties.

Finally, there are dozens of couples whom I interviewed but whose life stories do not appear in these chapters. I could never have done justice within the confines of this book's covers to the multitude of narratives I listened to, so my decision was to choose a group of highly representative pairs and examine their circumstances in depth and at length. I do hope that those couples whose interviews have not appeared here will nevertheless find themselves between the lines—as they should—for they have been essential to my thinking and they are truly present in these pages.

Acknowledgments

My first and most heartfelt thanks go to Dr. Patricia Papernow, my longtime pal and mentor, who has accompanied me every step of the way. Patricia is herself happily remarried and has thirty years of experience in the remarriage field under her belt. She is also a brilliant theorist whose influence is felt throughout this book.

I would also like to express my appreciation to the eminent sociologist Andrew J. Cherlin, Benjamin H. Griswold III Professor of Public Policy at Johns Hopkins University, as well as to Lawrence Ganong, Professor of Human Development and Family Studies at the University of Missouri; Kay Pasley, Department Chair and Norejane Hendrickson Professor, College of Human Sciences, Florida State University and stepfamily expert council member at the National Stepfamily Resource Center; D'Vera Cohn, Senior Writer at the Pew Research Center; Robert Klopfer, LCSW, Director of the Stepping Stones Counseling Center in Ridgewood, New Jersey; Monica McGoldrick, MSW, PhD, Director of the Multicultural Family Institute in Highland Park, New Jersey; Dr. Jeannette Lofas, Director of the Stepfamily Foundation; Elizabeth Einstein, MA, LMFT, stepfamily educator; James Merrell, architect; Dr. Margorie Engel, stepfamily money-management expert; Joanne Bickel, financial expert with a special focus on women's issues; Attorney Leslie E. Grodd, MBA,

ACKNOWLEDGMENTS

JD; and family court judge E. Chouteau Levine, among others too numerous to mention. A special note of thanks goes to the members of the first remarried couples' group I attended: I appreciate your letting me be there.

Finally, when it comes to saying thank you to my gifted and ingenious editor, Shannon Welch, and to Scribner Editor-in-Chief Nan Graham—who saw what this author's manuscript needed in an eyeblink—I am rendered almost speechless. All that I can say is that in my long career as a published writer, I have never encountered this level of smarts and expertise. You two are truly very special people, and I am so lucky to have found you.

Maggie Scarf

Suggested Further Reading
and Resources

Bray, James H. and John Kelly. *Stepfamilies: Love, Marriage, and Parenting in the First Decade.* New York: Broadway Books, 1998.

Browning, Scott and Elise Artelt. *Stepfamily Therapy: A 10-Step Clinical Approach.* Washington, DC: American Psychological Association, 2012.

Burr, Mala S. and Roger B. Burr. *Stepfamilies: The Step By Step Model of Brief Therapy.* New York: Brunner/Mazel, Inc., 1996.

Faber, Adele and Elaine Mazlish, *How to Talk So Kids Will Listen & Listen So Kids Will Talk.* New York: Scribner, 2012.

Ganong, Lawrence H. and Marilyn Coleman. *Stepfamily Relationships: Development, Dynamics, and Interventions.* New York: Plenum Publishers, 2004.

Gottman, John. *Why Marriages Succeed or Fail: What You Can Learn from the Breakthrough Research to Make Your Marriage Last.* New York: Simon & Schuster, 1994.

Kahn, Sandra S. *The Ex-Wife Syndrome: Cutting the Cord and Breaking Free After the Marriage Is Over.* New York: Random House, 1990.

Lofas, Jeannette. *Family Rules: Helping Stepfamilies and Single Parents Build Happy Homes.* New York: Kensington Publishing Corp., 1998.

———. *Stepparenting: Everything You Need to Know to Make It Work.* New York: Kensington Publishing Corp., 2004.

Martin, Wednesday. *Stepmonster: A New Look at Why Real Stepmothers Think, Feel, and Act the Way We Do.* New York: Houghton Mifflin Harcourt, 2009.

Papernow, Patricia L. *Becoming a Stepfamily: Patterns of Development in Remarried Families.* Hillsdale, NJ: The Analytic Press, 1993.

Stewart, Susan D. *Brave New Stepfamilies: Diverse Paths Toward Stepfamily Living.* Thousand Oaks, CA: Sage Publications, Inc., 2007.

Stone, Douglas, Bruce Patton, and Sheila Heen. *Difficult Conversations: How to Discuss What Matters Most*. New York: Penguin Books, 2010.

Wittmann, Jeffrey P. *Custody Chaos, Personal Peace: Sharing Custody with an Ex Who Drives You Crazy*. New York: The Berkley Publishing Group, 2001.

Yalom, Marilyn and Laura L. Carstensen, eds. *Inside the American Couple: New Thinking, New Challenges*. Berkeley, CA: University of California Press, 2002.

National Stepfamily Resource Center: www.stepfamilies.info
Online resources and clearinghouse for stepfamily members and research.

Q&A with Maggie Scarf

Why do you think there has been so little widely accepted theory and therapeutic training to help couples navigate remarriage?

Beats me! Considering that an estimated 43 percent of all new marriages now contain at least one partner who has been married before, you would think that there would be much more focus on remarried families. But the problem is that most people have trouble wrapping their minds around the basic truth that first-time families and remarried families are profoundly different in nature. There seems to be a commonly shared belief that remarried families are the same as first-time families, aside from the fact that there is a new dad or mom in place—the stepparent. But it is not that simple.

I think it's this basic misconception that has led to the high rate of remarital breakups, which is believed to be at least 10 percent higher than the rate of first-marriage failures—that is, in the neighborhood of 60 percent.

Given that remarrying couples are usually older, wiser, and able to make more informed marital choices, why are remarriages statistically so much more perilous than first marriages?

Most new partners see remarriage as a fresh chance at happiness with the partner they should have chosen in the first place. But they are in love, and their expectations are lovingly unrealistic; they just don't anticipate the unique challenges that second families typically face. Among these are the children's loyalty binds, the breakdown of parenting tasks, and the uniting of disparate family cultures. These are three of the five major structural challenges of remarriage outlined by psychologist Patricia Papernow in her Architectural Model of remarriage. Essentially, the remarried family's difficult and completely unforeseen job is to leave behind many of their old assumptions about how a "real family"—i.e., a traditional, first-marriage family—is supposed to operate and get to work on self-consciously planning, designing, and building an entirely new kind of family structure that will meet their own unique requirements.

When a remarried pair runs into big problems, is it more helpful/successful to have individual or couples' therapy to address the difficulties?

The answer to this question depends on the situation. If a stepparent and stepchild are in an ongoing battle, this pair could see a therapist together. If the partners in a remarried couple are at each other's throats, they should be the ones in treatment. You have to determine who is impacting the system in the most troublesome way; it could even be an aunt or an in-law and the stepmom who are at odds. Above all, never start with the whole family in treatment. When everyone is together, you can bet that tensions will be at their highest. And another thing: try your best to find someone who is trained in working with remarried families. Therapists who use a first-family model are not really going to understand the complex issues that re-wedded couples face.

What are the most common types of discord the second time around? What are the subjects that reliably cause remarried couples to quarrel, and how can the partners anticipate and defuse thorny situations before they become too volatile?

Interestingly enough, in a first marriage the most common cause of discord is money, and the second-most common cause is children. In remarriage, that gets turned on its head: remarried couples argue most about children and second-most about finances. As far as defusing arguments is concerned, the best answers lie in the realm of interpersonal communication. This is especially true regarding matters that lie very close to the mates' hearts, like the sensitive issue of children's behavior. Are the members of the pair respectful of and caring for each other's youngsters, who have undergone difficult losses and transitions? Or does a stepparent respond to a child's unfriendliness with outrage and attack? To take one example, it is far better for a stepmom to say to her mate "I feel hurt when your daughters come to visit and don't even say hello to me or make eye contact" than it is to say "Whenever your bratty daughters come over, they walk right past me as if I didn't even exist! They are so rude, and you just stand there!" The first response is an "I" message and could start a useful discussion about how to handle the problem, while the second is a "you" response that is blaming and likely to provoke an argument.

Describe Patricia Papernow's Architectural Model. How did it inform your research?

Papernow's ingenious model is based on the important truth that first-marriage families and remarried families can be likened to two discrete buildings whose basic blueprints differ significantly. Everyone is of course familiar with the structure of the first-marriage family. Metaphorically speaking, it corresponds to the family most of us grew up in; it is the family that exists in our heads. But the design of the remarried family is relatively unknown, and few people even understand that it is constructed according to a fundamentally different design plan. The elemental difference between these two "buildings" is created by the crucial fact that biological parents have deep, long-standing connections to their blood-and-heart-related children and newcomer/stepparents do not.

This situation presents the family with a number of complex design issues that require them to discard what architects refer to as the "vernacular" or "conventional planning." The remarried couple and their children must leave behind many of their taken-for-granted assumptions about how a family structure is supposed to look. Since the new family is coming together when the adult parents are older, and one or both are bringing the children of former relationships into the mix, the family structure they build together will differ significantly from the more traditional first-marriage design. As a result, their assumptions about family organization must of necessity undergo the process of being dismantled, reanalyzed, and reconfigured in ways that will work well for their newly amalgamating group. This is where the notion of "architectural expertise" comes in.

This is only a brief statement about a long, subtle process of family reorganization. But let it be said that this crisp model provided me with an excellent framework when it came to interviewing a wide swath of remarried couples of differing ages, socioeconomic status, and ethnicities.

The five major challenges of remarriage are a central feature of the Architectural Model. Can you describe these challenges and give some examples from your book? Can you suggest some ways of meeting the challenges?

Sure. The first is *Insider/Outsider Forces.* Insider/Outsider Forces tend to shift the members of the couple into polar opposite positions. The outsider (the stepparent) is struggling to enter the family system and make some changes of her own. The insider (the biological parent) shares a deep, strong bond with his children, who are often highly resistant to the newcomer. So the outsider is struggling to become a real member of the family and feeling left out in the cold. The insider is carrying on a shuttle diplomacy between his new love and his old, deep bonds with his children. He or she is trying hard to mediate between the customary ways the family used to operate and the different ways his outsider partner feels it should operate now. The outsider often feels unwelcome, ignored, or downright invisible, while the insider often feels frustrated and exhausted. A glaring example of this situation occurred in the remarriage of Julie and Matthew Albright. Julie was never able to gain access to the family—to suggest changes, to have her parenting supported, to have any input in family decision making. She described herself as "some kind of family add-on," "an amorphous kind of being"—someone whose ways of parenting were constantly criticized and derided by Matthew and his ex-wife.

The remarriage did not survive.

So how does a couple best handle this situation? First and foremost, simply being aware of the impact of insider/outsider forces is a huge step toward resolving them. I would suggest several sessions during which the insider parent listens with empathy (and without interruptions) to the outsider's bewilderment, hurt feelings, and sense of being ostracized. Ideally, a day or so later, the insider can take the same uninterrupted and empathetic space of time (twenty minutes) to describe his or her frustrating attempts to be heard.

Both insider and outsider positions are stressful.

Another great tip is to avoid spending lots of time together as one big, not-so-happy family. Time with the whole new family together is time when tensions tend to be at their highest. Rather, spend a lot of one-to-one time: time shared by the bio-parent and each of his or her children, to keep the connection strong. Time with the stepparent and each of the new stepchildren, who need to establish a connection without the biological parent around. The stepparent might find some easy ways of connecting with his or her stepchildren—whether it is playing a board game, baking cookies, or having a teenager show him or her how to tweet.

Finally, and most importantly, the couple needs to set aside regular time to be alone—to go out to dinner, see a movie, or go for a hike—in order to keep the relationship positive and rewarding. The major point here is that establishing good *one-on-one connections* throughout the entire family is key to overcoming this challenge.

Children's Losses

The fact is that the biological parent's gain—a new romantic partner—is often experienced by his or her children as yet another in a series of family calamities. Remember that the stepchildren involved in remarriage situations have often undergone early losses and stressful transitions, such as a move out of the family home or a switch to a strange school. Also, the initial loss of the intact family—most likely due to divorce—has been experienced as a volcanic upheaval, inevitably bringing deep grief and fears of abandonment in its wake.

Moreover, the stepchildren are often struggling with loyalty issues: the guilty feeling that harboring liking—or even outright loving—feelings for the "replacement parent" is a betrayal of the "real," biological parent (in reality or, if that parent is dead, in memory).

What to do? It's helpful to limit the number of new rules and changes at the outset of the new marriage. What changes you do make should be minimal and focused on maintaining civility. For example, a stepchild should be required to look at the stepparent and say hello when entering a room rather than greeting the biological parent and pretending that this new person (the spouse) is not present.

For children who are struggling with loyalty issues, it's important to let them know that their "real" parent will always occupy a secure place in their heart. If they are wondering if it is a betrayal to start to love their stepparent, it is important to help them understand that she or he will occupy a different place in their heart. The important message is that the biological parent and the stepparent can exist in different places in a heart that is large enough to house both of them.

This brings to mind Abbie Jamison's ten-year-old son, who detested his gentle, tender-hearted stepfather, Owen. Rob resented the fact that his mother's marriage had involved a cascade of changes centered around a move across the country to Connecticut, which meant being torn away from his close circle of friends, cousins, and his beloved grandparents, who remained in California. In this case it took time—three whole years—for this situation to resolve in an unexpectedly happy ending.

Parenting Tasks

The parenting tasks faced by remarried couples tend to move partners into intense and opposing positions. Before the new marriage, the mate's single-parent family system has probably become too permissive, for, over time, families with this type of structure tend to become lax and to bend the rules. The stepparent wants to effect some changes and establish her or his authority, but the stepchildren ignore or defy his or her requests. They've suffered through too many demands for change already and want things to remain just as they were before she or he appeared upon the scene.

Is the bio-parent right to want to go easy on the children and their often disrespectful behavior? Is the stepparent right to insist on more deference and domestic order? One parent is too easygoing; the other responds by becoming more harsh. A ton of research has established that neither style is optimal when it comes to the children's development and growth. The best style of child-rearing is authoritative—firm yet loving, kind but setting clear limits on the child's behavior.

Disciplining stepchildren is a particularly charged issue in remarried families, especially if the parents are polarized in opposing (too soft/too hard) positions. So is it okay for a stepparent to punish the biological parent's child? The unequivocal answer is NO. Only the biological parent can mete out punishment, while the stepparent's role is more like that of a monitor, nanny, or aunt—he or she is in charge while the biological parent is absent, but is not entitled to punish misbehavior. The stepparent reports back about any misbehavior and lets the spouse decide if and how to punish.

A case in point is Bruce Gray, who adored his stepdaughter, Trisha. Trisha had lived with him since the age of five. Her natural father was on the scene only rarely, so Bruce felt as if he was her real dad. But when Trisha was almost twelve years old, she became fresh, nasty, and oppositional. Bruce lost patience with her one day and got so angry that he took her over his knee and spanked her. Trish was outraged. "You're not my real dad!" Bruce's stepdaughter declared—words that pierced him to the core. Although the Grays' remarriage was a success in every other way, Bruce's relationship with his beloved stepdaughter never recovered. And he still mourned this years later.

Of course an underlying dilemma is that the biological parent often *has* become lax and overly permissive and needs to firm up, while the stepparent needs to show more patience and compassion. Communicating with each other in a way that is respectful and caring is important. Here, a skill called "soft-hard-soft" can be very helpful. Since parents are hypersensitive when it comes to their ways of child-rearing, the stepparent begins with a soft, affectionate message: "You know how deeply I care about Trisha." Then, like a sandwich filling, comes the harder message: "But she is being so rude and disagreeable that I'm sometimes on the verge of losing my temper." Finally, the communication ends with another soft message: "You know how much I adore Trisha, so how can we handle this? When she tries to get my goat, what's your advice about what I should do?"

The Uniting of Two Disparate Family Cultures

One of the biggest challenges for remarried couples and their children is the uniting of two very different family cultures. Each party brings a history and hundreds of familiar habits, rules, and routines to the newly created stepfamily. Agreement on everything from whether you can start eating before everyone sits down at the table to whether you hang your coat on a hook or throw it on the sofa to how much TV is permissible is simply taken for granted by the biological parent and the children. But these rhythms of being are unknown and not understood by the newest member of the family.

The difficulties that emerge in this situation have to do with the relatively thin common ground shared by the remarried partners and the thick common ground forged over the years by the biological parent and his or her offspring. The newly married couple has not had long to work out their own differences, agreements, and easy pathways to action. A new and different common ground must be created over the course of time, one that includes all members of the new family system.

To cite an example, before remarrying, Carol Burke had explained to her live-in adult stepchildren that she would not intrude on their privacy in their wing of the house. But she did ask that in the shared kitchen they put the dishes in the dishwasher, dry the pots and pans and put them away, and take out the trash. However, her husband, Ted's, children simply ignored her requests and left the sink full of dishes and the wastebasket overflowing. Her laid-back, permissive husband kept insisting that this created no real problem; the difficulty was all "in Carol's own mind." She was feeling increasingly invisible and ignored—an alien in a strange land. Indeed, Carol feared that she might in fact be going crazy.

As any remarriage gets underway, a host of unanticipated issues suddenly come up for discussion, and the opportunities for hurt and distress are legion. The new couple must understand that they need to work in tandem to negotiate the changing mores of daily life. In the Burkes' instance, Ted needed to understand how shut out of the family system Carol was feeling, while Carol needed to understand Ted's frustration as he tried to placate both his new bride and his children.

The Burkes' story took some highly unusual twists and turns.

In more commonplace situations in which younger children are involved, the best advice is to focus initially on what is vitally important, such as safety and civility. Also, reassure the children about what familiar parts of their routine are going to stay the same.

The Extension of Family Boundaries

In a first-marriage nuclear family, the members include the biological parents and their blood-related, dependent children. In the case of remarriage, the new household will not be complete as it stands, for there will be a family member living outside it (the other biological parent) who must be included within the overall system. Therefore, there will be need to be a "boundary with a hole in it" to offer this parent easy access. This unclosed boundary can be fraught with difficulties.

The new spouse may resent how much time the biological parent spends on the phone with his ex-wife gabbing about the children's plans and schedules. It is now time to set a clear barrier with the ex-spouse that makes it easy to facilitate issues and schedules relating to the children but closes the door to spending time on interpersonal issues and engaging in long, friendly chit-chats.

There are two major ways in which the outside biological parent can present a major obstacle to the success of the new marriage. One is called "the bondage of caring." This is a situation in which the ex-spouse remains emotionally dependent upon the former mate. A glaring example of this was seen in the case of the Albrights. Matthew's first wife became second-wife Julie's "new best friend"; she undermined Julie's parenting of her stepson and even called ex-husband Matthew up eight years after his remarriage to tell him she still loved him and cherished their relationship. She had never left the remarried Albrights' domestic scene.

Another way that the other biological parent can create turmoil in the remarriage is known as "the bondage of bitterness." In this case, the ex-spouse has remained linked to her or his former mate by an emotional connection that is hot, angry, and destructive. This was certainly obvious in the instance of the happily remarried Duvaliers. Cliff's ex-wife, Lorraine, had run off with her lover and later married him, leaving Cliff shaken to the core and in a state of emotional paralysis. Lorraine had supposed that Cliff was her property and that he would grieve for her forever. Therefore, his joyful relationship to new wife Sara—and his clear-cut indifference to Lorraine—were developments that Lorraine found deeply insulting and enraging. She did her best to cause weekly upsets in the new marriage, but met with no success.

What about the more mundane kinds of issues that can arise when the children of remarriage are rotating between two different households where the folkways are very different? Perhaps the kids can have Coke at Mom's house but only milk in the remarried couple's home. Here, a helpful metaphor to present to the children is this: "Having two houses, like Mom's house and Dad's house, is like having two different teachers. In Mrs. Smith's class you have to raise your hand to even sharpen a pencil. In Mr. Jones's class you can walk around anytime you please." This is a low-key way of saying that different households can adhere to their own ways of operating without implying that one is better than the other. They are just different, and that is okay.

What are the kinds of money issues that may arise in remarriage? What is meant by the one, two, or three-pot method of handling finances in a remarried household?

I'll respond to the second part of this question first:

Differences about money often become a freighted issue in remarried families, and a good strategy for finessing these problems is known as the "three-pot solution." Couples who work out this form of compromise keep three separate accounts. One is held jointly by the two partners and is used for the running of the household, including repairs, food bills, and so forth. Another account contains the wife's savings and income and is used to cover her own expenses and those of her children. A third account is maintained by the husband and is designated for his private expenses and those of his children.

Other partners decide to keep separate accounts and handle all child-rearing and household expenses on a fifty-fifty basis. Obviously, this is a "two-pot" arrangement.

Still another method of handling finances is when partners simply pool all their financial resources together. This is the "one-pot" solution to managing the new household's money, and it is usually done in an effort to ensure rapid blending.

The money issues that may arise in remarriage are surprisingly numerous. They include pensions, social security, insurance benefits, and many others. The new spouse needs to know the answer to the question *"Financially speaking, what happens to me if something unexpected and catastrophic happens to my new partner?"*

What is the best advice you can give a couple about to remarry?

Even though you are in love, arm yourself with information about remarriage, so that your expectations of what lies ahead will be realistic. Then you will not be blindsided. Also, have that all-important conversation about financial resources, yours and his. This will be the best wedding gift you can give to each other—the gift of openness and trust.

About the Author

Maggie Scarf is a former visiting fellow at the Whitney Human-
ities Center, Yale University, and a current fellow of Jonathan
Edwards College, Yale University. She was for many years a contributing editor to *The New Republic* and a member of the advisory
board of the American Psychiatric Press.

Maggie Scarf is the author of six books for adults, including
the acclaimed *New York Times* bestsellers *Unfinished Business: Pres-
sure Points in the Lives of Women* and *Intimate Partners: Patterns in
Love and Marriage*. Her other books include *Body, Mind, Behav-
ior* (a collection of essays originally published in *The New York
Times Magazine*); *Intimate Worlds: How Families Thrive and Why
They Fail*; *Secrets, Lies, Betrayals: How the Body Holds the Secrets of a
Life, and How to Unlock Them*; and, most recently, *September Songs:
The Good News About Marriage in the Later Years*. She is also the
author of two books for children.

Ms. Scarf is the recipient of numerous awards and fellowships,
including a Ford Foundation Fellowship and a Nieman Fellowship in Journalism at Harvard University. She has received several National Media Awards from the American Psychological
Foundation. Ms. Scarf has served on the National Commission
on Women and Depression, received a Certificate of Appreciation
from the Connecticut Psychological Association, and received the
Connecticut United Nations Award, citing her as an Outstanding

Connecticut Woman. In 1997, she was awarded a Special Certificate of Commendation from the American Psychiatric Association for an article on patient confidentiality ("Keeping Secrets") published in *The New York Times Magazine*.

She has appeared on CNN and on many television programs, including *The Oprah Winfrey Show,* the *Today Show, Good Morning America,* and *CBS News,* and has been interviewed extensively on radio and for magazines and newspapers across the nation. She currently blogs for *Psychology Today*.

Maggie Scarf lives in Connecticut with her husband, Herb, the Sterling Professor of Economics at Yale, and is the mother of three daughters.

Printed in the United States
By Bookmasters